45 Years into the
WILDERNESS

William C. Kriner

Copyright © 2011 William C. Kriner
All rights reserved.

Front Cover Photo: Graduation Day, Class of 1965, DuBois Area High School

Back Cover Photo: Danny Showers and Jack Royer at Jack's Wedding where Danny served as Best Man (Courtesy of Royer Family)

ISBN-10: 1466262745
EAN-13: 9781466262744

Contents

Preface and Dedication 1
Introduction. 7
Mighty, Mighty Seniors 11
The Ensuing Chaos 29
Why the Chaos? Connecting the Dots 43
We Are All Modern People 55
Let Me Introduce You to Postmodernism, the New Us 63
The New Society. 69
A Time for Reassessment. 91
What Now? 107
Epilogue 113
Appendix A 123
Appendix B. 125
Bibliography. 129

Preface and Dedication

Legend has it that they met in the hospital. Danny was born on October 9, 1947, and Jack was born two days earlier, on October 7, 1947. I first met them in Little League. Danny played for Triangle Springs, Jack for Shaw Trucking, and I for bottom-dweller DuBrook. Jack was a tiger at third base, and Danny played shortstop. I played second base, but as a rotund preteen, I could not compete with them in baseball.

They were both all-stars in 1960. Because of my birthday, my Little League experience ended in 1959, but I still recall going to see them play the next year. By that time we had become good friends in the seventh grade at the Scribner Avenue Junior High School. From that point on in our schooling, one or both of them was in my homeroom and both of them in my section for classes.

Jack was from the typical middle-class family found in DuBois in the 1950s. He was one of four children (the four Js) and the only boy. He was raised on the East Side of DuBois, which was really the north side of the city. He attended his neighborhood school on Second Avenue. Danny was raised by a single mom—his dad died when he was two—and lived on Main Street near the DuBois Brewery. He attended school in Falls Creek, another neighborhood school, where his mother taught the fourth grade.

Both Jack and Danny were excellent students and had loads of friends. Because Danny was an only child and Jack an only son, and because my brother was nine years older than I, in many ways we were to one another the brothers we never had. We all had loving families, attended church and participated in church activities (Danny at St. Catherine's, Jack at Lebanon Lutheran, and me at First Methodist), knew right from wrong, and most of the time practiced the Golden Rule. We had many adventures together and managed to stay out of juvenile court. After six years of schooling, we graduated in June of 1965, ready, so we believed, to face the world.

Jack started with me at Penn State, which was the beginning of an academic career for him. He obtained a BS in forest technology (with honors) from Penn State in 1969. While in the U.S. Army, working

Preface and Dedication

on the White House detail, he studied at American University and in 1973 was awarded an MS in environmental systems management. He then pursued a PhD in natural resources, which he earned from Cornell University in 1980. Early on in his career, he married Patty on August 28, 1970, at St. Joseph's Church in Aliquippa, Pennsylvania. Danny served as his best man. Jack and Patty had two children, Katie, born in 1981, and Michael, born in 1985.

Jack taught at Duke University from 1978 to 1987, with the last two years as the acting director of Duke's Center for Resource and Environmental Policy. He was lured back to Pennsylvania to become the Director of Academic Affairs at the Fayette Campus of Penn State in 1987. In 1989, he went to Main Campus first as Associate Dean for Undergraduate Education and finally as Senior Associate Dean, Commonwealth Education System.

Danny went on to St. Francis, where he earned a BA in business in 1969. He entered the U.S. Army on January 1970 and served in army intelligence until his discharge in December of 1972. On October 10, 1970, he married Joan and together they had two daughters, Jessica, born in 1972, and Katie, born in 1975. After discharge, Danny went to work for Moore Business Forms. He and his family lived in

45 Years into the Wilderness

Columbia, Maryland, near Washington DC. During this time, the Shower and Royer families were able to spend a lot of time together.

Danny was offered a job with Willamette Industries in Indianapolis, where he became sales manager. After eight years, he was asked to oversee the construction of a new plant for the company in Rock Hill, South Carolina, near Charlotte. He became general manager of the plant with fifty people reporting to him. After moving to North Carolina, Danny and Joan hoped to be reunited with the Royers, but Jack had already accepted the job at Penn State.

Jack was unexpectedly taken from our midst on July 17, 1997, the fiftieth birthday of his very best East Side buddy and our high school classmate, Dan Kohlhepp. It was a shock to the Penn State community and to all who knew Jack. I was trying a case out of town, and when I returned to hear the news of Jack's death, I could not believe it. I had not seen Jack since he was at Duke. It was incomprehensible to me that I would never speak to him again. No one was prepared for his death.

In 1991, Danny developed ocular melanoma, but he never lost his upbeat attitude about life. Around this time, I last talked to Danny, and I sensed his

Preface and Dedication

will to be an overcomer. He had his eye nucleated at Duke University and was pronounced cured, but in September of 1997, cancer returned to his liver. He had rigorous and extensive treatment at the MD Anderson Treatment Center, but on June 2, 1998, he met his Maker. He, as we all do, desired to live to see his children's children. Much of his treatment was experimental and difficult, but he showed great courage and bravery, even in the face of death. He was a man of great Christian faith and while on his deathbed was surrounded by individuals praying prayers of intercession for him.

Both Jack and Dan were highly respected by their colleagues. In September of 1997, the month Danny's cancer returned, the Center for Learning and Academic Technologies at Penn State was renamed the Jack P. Royer Center for Learning and Academic Technologies. After Danny's death, his employer, Willamette Industries, presented the Medical University of South Carolina with a thirty thousand dollar check in Danny's name and memory during a ceremony Joan and their daughters attended.

This book is about what has happened to our culture since the graduation of the class of '65. A lot of it is not pretty. I dedicate this book to Jack and Danny because I would like to have them around today to help us all find our way through what has been characterized as "the age of the empty self." Jack and Dan were men, grown-ups who knew about responsibility to family, their work, and society. They understood that the world did not exist for them. In the words of one of their widows, they were "kind, caring, moral, responsible, and loving." We need more, not fewer, men like them.

There is remorse in this dedication too. As I look back at my life and theirs, I see how I have succumbed to the spirit of the age. I was a lousy friend to Jack and Danny. I was caught up in career and work that seemed good at the time. At what cost? I missed out on a relationship with two men who were, and could have remained, wonderful influences in my life. In my reflections over the last ten years on what happened to the culture since the class of '65, I have thought often of Jack and Danny. So, this is for you, guys. It's a more difficult world without you, but I am determined and committed to doing what I can to make it better. I never got to say this to you: Thanks for who you were and what you did for many, including me.

Introduction

I graduated from high school in June of 1965, in the midst of the decade of the sixties. Much has been written about that ten-year period and its impact. This is an attempt to examine the period from 1965 to 2010, a total of forty-five years, by one who lived through that time period. This is not an academic book, but rather a common-sense examination of those four and one-half decades.

I begin by looking at the national and international events of 1964–65, leading up to graduation in June of 1965 as they would have been mediated to high school students in small-town USA. From there, I look at the revolutionary turmoil that was the sixties and the changes in the ensuing decades. I try to place a finger on the pulse of the social and cultural history that resulted from what was begun in the sixties, and I witness to the precepts inherited from the revolutions of that time that dictate how we live today. Finally, I outline remedies for individuals for overcoming the confusion and seeming helplessness of living in the society of today rooted in the sixties.

45 Years into the Wilderness

In case some are skeptical about changes since the decade of the sixties, let's examine some facts. Starting in 1964, average SAT scores went steadily down.

From 1960 to 1993, the average SAT score dropped 75 points! During the same thirty-three year period, violent crime increased 560 percent! In 1965, 7.7 percent of all births were out of wedlock and 73 percent of all households were made up of married couples. By 2000, however, out-of-wedlock births amounted to 33 percent of all births and only 52 percent of all households were made up of married couples. I am not presenting these to prove some sort of social point, but to indicate that Stephen Stills was correct in singing, "Something's happening here."

The next line of that song, "What it is ain't exactly clear," is what I try to address in this book. No doubt something happened in the 1960s. Some even believe they know what it was. Yet largely unexamined is the proposition that the society in which we all find ourselves is the result of the what, how, and why of the forty-five years beginning in 1965. Causes of the sixties' uprisings as well as the benefit of any changes, continue to be debated. Little doubt remains, however, that traditional views of

Introduction

institutions, individuals, community, and authority have changed since then.

I write this book not to engage in those debates or to make a plea for the way it used to be. My hope is that this book will assist readers in recognizing that changes did occur that affected us all, whether we knew it or not. I also hope that readers will recognize that we need not acquiesce to the changes cultural and societal forces of this age seek to impose on us. A better way to live may be achieved on a person-by-person basis. It is a way that does not turn back the clock, but recaptures a sense of unchangeable human nature, situated in family and community, based on standards rather than founded on the desires of man.

If you lived through the sixties, had parents or grandparents who did, or have heard so much about the era that you want to get a better idea of the what, where, and why, this book is for you. I call this firsthand account and analysis *45 Years into the Wilderness*—the forty-five years from 1965 to 2010. What society is like now and beyond owes much to what occurred in this forty-five-year period with its genesis in the 1960s. May the reader gain an understanding of the tumultuous sixties and their consequences and how they impact the reader today. May it also assist each of us to live a life of full human flourishing seeking the highest good.

WCK
February 19, 2011

Mighty, Mighty Seniors

It was August 31, 1964, the beginning of the 1964–65 school year in the DuBois Area School District. Enrollment totaled 4,226 students.[1] For the class of 1965, this day marked the beginning of the last year in public school. Most of the students had attended eleven or twelve years of school before this, their final year of schooling financed by taxpayers and required by law.

It was an exciting day for the class of '65. Like all "mighty, mighty seniors" they were looking forward to the last year of school at the top of the school population pecking order. They would soon be graduating and moving on to bigger and better things. For now, however, the classmates were going to enjoy the year with school activities and social events that they wanted to be fun and memorable. Yet, rumbling

---

1 All factual references came from the local newspaper of DuBois, *The Courier-Express*, unless noted otherwise.

45 Years into the Wilderness

beneath the surface of the culture were cataclysmic changes soon to explode. The class of '65 was oblivious to them all. While they knew the sun-splashed world of fun and games would change as they became adults, they were certainly unprepared for the tsunami of change that would redefine the world in which they lived.

Several ongoing societal battles were occurring in the late summer of 1964 that continued into the senior year of the class of '65. The August 31 edition of the newspaper carried an article originating from Mt. Sterling, Kentucky. It recounted how a Negro Masonic Lodge as well as an all-Negro school, ironically named the Dubois School, had been razed by fire. This apparent fire bombing was in reaction to the integration of Kentucky public schools. In the summer of 1964, Negro was still the word of choice to describe African Americans in a non derogatory fashion. Take for example the main headline on the August 17, 1964 newspaper: THOUSAND NEGROES RIOT NEAR CHICAGO; 50 HURT. This headline reflected the ongoing struggle known as the Civil Rights Movement facing the nation.

During the summer of 1964 the Council of Federated Organizations (COFO) sent one thousand students and teachers to Mississippi to train,

Mighty, Mighty Seniors

organize, and register Negroes to vote. These Freedom Riders were on the front lines of the Civil Rights Movement. James Chaney, Michael Schwerer, and Andrew Goodman were three of the summer volunteers. They were working in Neshoba County, Mississippi. On June 21, 1964, they were arrested and, after a brief time, allegedly turned over to the local KKK. Their bodies later were found in Philadelphia, Mississippi. A nationwide outrage ensued, which some cynics attribute to the fact that two of the victims were white. These shocking slayings brought home to the country the extent of violent opposition to the African American vote and the integration of schools. For the seniors of DuBois High School, however, the rights of Negroes seemed like a problem in a foreign land. With no Negroes in the school, no personal awareness of the issues existed. We seemed nothing more than spectators.

In January of 1965, daily marches began in Selma, Alabama. The Civil Rights Act had become law but to black folks in the South it was incomplete. In order to get the law passed, a deal was struck to omit voting rights from the act. So, Dr. Martin Luther King decided Selma was the place to continue the struggle for voting rights. Selma had a majority of black residents but only 3 percent were registered

45 Years into the Wilderness

to vote. So, what white folk thought may have ended with the 1964 law continued and escalated.

On February 18, 1965 Jimmy Lee Jackson was killed by police in nearby Marion, Alabama. In response to Jackson's death, the Southern Christian Leadership Council organized a protest march from Selma to Birmingham, Alabama's capital. Governor Wallace banned the march, and King urged it to be postponed until the federal government could step in to protect marchers from violence. The Student Nonviolent Coordinating Committee would not back down, however, and the march was held on March 7. At the Edmund Pettus Bridge leading into Montgomery, the marchers were viciously attacked by police. The images were flashed all over America and journalists dubbed the carnage "Bloody Sunday." Most agree that this debacle was the turning point in the embracing of the Civil Rights Movement by the majority of Americans.

Four days later, J. J. Reeb, a white minister from Boston, died from a beating inflicted by an anti-black gang in Selma. The White House was under increasing pressure to do something to stop the death and injury. On March 15, President Johnson announced he would be sending a voting rights bill to Congress. He lifted the ban on the march interrupted on

Mighty, Mighty Seniors

March 7 and the march went off without violence to Birmingham. The Voting Rights Act became law on August 3, 1965. Unbeknownst to the class of '65, the Civil Rights struggle taking place during their senior year of high school would have impacts on them for years to come.

A societal change resisted at the local level was the U.S. Supreme Court's beginning assault on the public expression of religion, particularly Christianity. The class of '65 had gone through school with daily Bible reading and prayer, usually the Lord's Prayer. The Court in two separate decisions, *Engle v. Vitale*, 370 US 421 (1962) and *School District of Abington v. Schempp*, 374 US 203 (1963), had ruled prayer, including recitation of the Lord's Prayer, and Bible reading in public schools as a Constitutional violation. Curiously, the School Board of the DuBois Area School District ignored the advice of their solicitor Dave Blakely to cease the practices of prayer and Bible reading before class. The Board tabled action to abide by the decisions and permitted teachers to continue with prayer and Bible reading as their individual conscience dictated. In the August 18 edition of the *Courier-Express*, one teacher is quoted as saying: "I asked the students if they wanted it [prayer and Bible reading] and they said 'Yes'."

45 Years into the Wilderness

A nationwide uproar erupted over this movement of the Court against religion in the name of "separation of church and state." The Court had decoupled the dominant belief system in the country (Christianity) from government-sponsored schools. Protests against the Court's decisions were mostly wide of the mark. No one could seriously argue that the reading of Scripture and the praying of the Lord's Prayer was sufficient for the raising up of young people to be Christians. The decisions marked, however, the beginning of a public policy that placed religious belief in the private sphere. Over the years, there has been increased effort to eliminate the symbolism and tradition of Christianity from the public square and thereby further privatize belief. This has made it much easier, with the cultural development herein discussed, for folks to discard religious belief as a manifestation of the outmoded institutions of the past.

The third issue affecting America during the final year of high school for the class of '65 was the Vietnam conflict. While John Kennedy usually escapes criticism regarding Vietnam, he actually began the escalation that lead to the quagmire. During his presidency, short as it was, U.S. troop numbers went from seven hundred to over sixteen thousand.

Mighty, Mighty Seniors

Two years earlier, when the seniors were sophomores, in 1963, two incidents were indicative of the difficulties faced in the country. On June 11, 1963, the Venerable Thich Quang Duc doused himself with gasoline and lit a match. The image of his self immolation was shown over and over on television. His death reminded the world of the distrust the Buddhists had for the government of Premier Ngo Dinh Diem.

The second incident involved Diem himself. The U.S. government decided Diem was a liability and had to go. On November 1, 1963, South Vietnamese Air Force officers kidnapped their premier. His body was found in the back of a U.S. armored personnel carrier. Less than three weeks later, Kennedy himself was dead. These three deaths, a Buddhist monk, the premier of the country the United States was trying to protect, and the leader of the U.S. government who was groping for a plan and solution…ushered in a further chaotic time and additional failed policies of confusion.

Replacements for Diem were bigger stooges and even more ruthless. By the summer of 1964, when the class of '65 was gearing up for its big year, many close to the problem believed the regime would not last to January 1965. In August 1964, however, the

45 Years into the Wilderness

U.S. destroyer *Maddox* was fired upon, and the *Turner Jay*, another destroyer, spotted a torpedo attack. President Johnson insisted that he wanted no wider war. Nevertheless, he asked Congress on August 4 for the authority to "repel armed attack" against U.S. forces "to prevent further aggression" remaining until the President determines that "peace and security of the region is reasonably secured."[2] This was the infamous Tonkin Gulf Resolution.

As classes began for the class of '65, events revealed that nothing much had changed for the better. On August 31, an escalation of Roman Catholic/Buddhist unrest spawned new riots. These were blamed on the Communists, as reflected in the headline: BLAME COMMIES FOR VIET RELIGIOUS RIOTS. On September 14, it was reported that a coup against the premier of Vietnam had failed. The testing of Chinese Communist nuclear weapons and the implications for Viet Nam was reported on September 30. On October 7 a helicopter with five American soldiers aboard was shot down over Vietnam. In December, Buddhist monks went on a hunger strike to protest the government, the military threatened a takeover, and the United States demanded a civil authority in South Vietnam.

---

2 *New York Times*, August 5, 1964.

Mighty, Mighty Seniors

The war was going badly on the ground. The People's Liberation Armed Forces [PLAF or Viet Cong (VC)] were conducting vicious terror strikes in the south without any reprisals. President Johnson was reluctant to strike back because 1964 was an election year. While the regime in the south held on through the New Year, it seemed in early 1965 that Hanoi was on the threshold of victory. The VC stepped up its attacks on the U.S. military. On February 7, the VC attacked the base at Pleiku, killing nine. LBJ finally responded with Operation Flaming Dart, a bombing offensive against the North. Three days later, however, the VC attacked the Ohi Nhon base, killing twenty-three American soldiers. To his breaking point, Johnson ordered Operation Rolling Thunder, a sustained bombing campaign intended to destroy the VC. He also ordered the 9th Marine Expeditionary Brigade to hit the beaches northwest of Da Nang on March 9.

The bombing campaigns also engaged an air war. In April of 1965, Navy warplanes tangled with Soviet MIGS. Increased in-theater participation by Marines led to more fighting and therefore to more casualties. During May, U.S. troops took part in heavy fighting. The fighting gradually moved closer to the Cambodian/Vietnam border because the VC had retreated to Cambodia. As the violence escalated in Vietnam, no one in the class of '65 knew that many of its young men would serve, die, and be adversely affected by the conflict.

There was inevitability in all that was happening. Administration spokesmen trotted out the "domino theory" to justify the increasing presence in Vietnam, a chorus that would be repeated through the years. In April of 1965, Robert McNamara voiced his opinion that failure in Vietnam would shift world power to the Communists. In May, the Chinese detonated their second nuclear weapon, lending credence to the claim that a Communist hegemony would result in Southeast Asia if the United States did not prevail in Vietnam. Of course, the Vietnam "problem" was well known, if not understood. As the school year wore on, it became clear that the complexities of Vietnam were going to play a major role in U.S. politics and in the lives of all young people, including the class of '65.

A fourth issue was changing the landscape of America. It was tied to and empowered to some extent by what was occurring in Vietnam. This was the newfound liberation of American youth, coupled with a desire for a voice in the political activities of the United States. The parents of 1960s youth had grown up knowing war, depression, responsibility, and sacrifice. For instance, my father graduated from Brady Township High School on a Friday in May of 1936 and the next Monday was working as a deep miner at the Helvetia Deep Mine. He married the following March. His was a life of hard work and sacrifice to raise his family.

The baby boomer generation was liberated from those strictures by the affluence afforded by post-World War II effort and the thrift of their parents. This liberation did not occur without the consent of their parents. Baby boomer parents did not want their children to have to deal with the difficulties they endured. They envisioned a better life, albeit an undefined ideal, for their children. With perfect hindsight we can say that parents did not bargain for the revolt from parental beliefs/ideals that resulted from the excesses flowing from this liberation.

While sex, drugs, and lifestyle differences are trumpeted in popular literature as the keys to the '60s revolt, there was a deeper current running. C. Wright Mills, a champion of what became the '60s radicals, referred to what was happening as the Age of Complacency Ending.[3] I can vividly recall that my

---

3 C. Wright Mills in *New Left Review*, Sept-Oct, 1960.

45 Years into the Wilderness

brothers' contemporaries of the middle to late 1950s were criticized by adults as being "shallow young people" for stuffing themselves into Volkswagens and phone booths. In the '60s, those same critical adults aimed their dissatisfaction at young folks who were serious about the political direction of the country and protested about the Vietnam conflict. "Why can't they just lighten up?" they asked. There has always been schizophrenia for adults when dealing with the behavior of youth.

Pretty clearly, young people in the '60s were rebelling against authority. Not just parental authority, but all authority. The class of '65 fit the profile for youngsters that adults wanted at the time. They were wrapped up in being high school students, by and large, responsible and reasonable kids. It was the norm in DuBois, Pennsylvania, in 1964 and 1965. In the midst of such normalcy, one very important event occurred in the middle of football season in 1964 that would have a far reaching impact on all youth then and now. It was the Free Speech Movement (FSM).

On October 1, 1964, at the corner of Bancroft and Telegraph at the edge of the campus of the University of California at Berkeley, the FSM began. The Berkeley administration, taking its *parens parenti* responsibility seriously, banned political speech and participation by students in political events (read "protests") on the plot of land at that corner. The students, who could die in Vietnam, were not permitted to join in the debate on Vietnam. The students wanted the right to protest politically. So, in defiance of the administration they gathered. The police came and the students sat down blocking the cars using a tactic learned from the civil rights protestors.

Mario Savio jumped onto a police cruiser (after politely removing his shoes!) and exhorted for rights of expression on behalf of the students.[4] Savio then led the students to occupy Sproul Hall on the campus until their demands were met by the administration. The occupation ended on December 3, when Governor Edmund Brown ordered eight hundred demonstrators arrested. The students were granted their freedom of expression and limits on all types of political expression were removed. Students everywhere were emboldened. They asked: "Why couldn't the administration have done this in the beginning?"

---

4 Peter Levy, *America in the Sixties: Left, Right and Center*. Westport, CN: Greenwood Publishing, 1998, 38.

45 Years into the Wilderness

Today, the actions of the Cal authorities seem foolish. At the time, however, children were to be seen not heard. Just look at our world today. Young people hold economic, political, and social influence they never possessed or envisioned in the '60s. Berkeley during the senior year of the class of '65 changed everything for young people. After Berkeley, students began to protest any and all restrictions and sought total control over their lives. When the changes did not come as rapidly as they desired, anger was directed at all authorities seen as corrupt and repressive.

The easiest target for all protesting was the U.S. government's handling of Vietnam. It represented sending young people to die without their say for a cause that was futile, unnecessary, and unpopular. Campus unrest became the norm around the country after Berkeley. The biggest protest during the class of 1965's senior year was, of course, at Berkeley on May 21, 1965. It was billed as a twenty-four-hour Vietnam protest and drew ten thousand participants. The leader was Jerry Rubin who, unlike the thoughtful and shoeless Savio, ignored respectability and began the unsightly protests that drove wedges more deeply between the generations. In a few short months, the Free Speech Movement

Mighty, Mighty Seniors

became a playground for kooks, self promoters, and those who sought destruction of the entire system.

The FSM devolved into a protest against the very country and system that permitted it to happen in the first place, but in northwest Pennsylvania it gained no traction with those in the class of '65. Yet the day was coming when protesting born of the FSM would capture the attention of everyone with the 1968 riots at the Democratic National Convention in Chicago and the "four dead in O-hio" at Kent State University. The ground was moving under the feet of the class of '65 but few noticed the tremors. In time, no one would be able to ignore it.

In 1964, amid the building cultural turmoil surrounding civil rights, religious rights, Vietnam, and the youth liberation movement, a presidential election occurred. Barry Goldwater ran against Lyndon Baines Johnson (LBJ), the latter running as an incumbent by virtue of succeeding John F. Kennedy. LBJ had survived a primary battle with Hubert Humphrey and Goldwater was the first "real conservative" to run for president in the modern era. His slogan "In your heart you know he's right" was countered by his detractors with "In your guts you know he's nuts." LBJ pledged to bring about the "Great Society." He also asserted there would be no further

45 Years into the Wilderness

war in Vietnam after retaliation for alleged attacks on warships in the Gulf of Tonkin.

LBJ won 61.1 percent of the popular vote (43,129,484) taking forty-four states as well as the District of Columbia, and capturing 486 electoral votes.[5] The country was not ready for Goldwater and they believed in LBJ. Of course, history tells us that the war LBJ promised not to expand took him down; the Great Society, based on the outlandish rationale that the national government could end injustice and poverty for all its people, did not pan out; and many ideas espoused by Goldwater became the currency of successful campaigns from 1972 to the present day. What the seniors at DuBois High School observed in the current events of 1964–65 had consequences and impacts far beyond the unfolding events.

The class of '65 was playing or cheering for the Beavers and attending school with one eye on the future, a future that was not as it appeared. They lived the daily life of a teenager in small-town America, listening to the British Invasion led by the Beatles and singing and dancing to Motown tunes. These were kids, who would soon be adults and

---
5 *Dictionary of American History*, 3:165.

high school graduates, leaving behind their youthful years in DuBois, Pennsylvania. There was certainly an awareness of the "Vietnam problem." The military draft was an issue for all able-bodied young men, but attending college provided a draft deferment and fighting in faraway rice paddies could be avoided. Those not attending college sought enlistment in less problematic branches of the military.

Those with older siblings in college were aware of the new openness and demand for change that dawned on college campuses. For the most part, however, there was only a passing acknowledgement of what was going on outside of DuBois. Cafeteria table talk did not revolve around civil rights, free speech, war, and changes in cultural mores and standards. Whatever was happening seemed far removed from daily life and future plans.

On June 6, 1965, 334 students graduated from DuBois Area High School. It was a partly cloudy day as the class of '65 walked forward to receive their diplomas on the football field of what is now called Mansell Stadium. It was a time of hope and excitement for the future. The conversations of the graduates naturally centered on congratulations and good wishes. It all seemed so perfect, just as the parents had planned for their baby boomer children and as the children themselves had desired. No one noticed the gathering storm clouds of cultural change on the horizon or that the landscape of America was about to change forever. How and why did that happen?

The Ensuing Chaos

The forty-five years that followed the graduation of the class of '65 were chaotic. Little did the members of the class know, they were entering the world of the Seismic Sixties, which represented a sharp break with the Golden Fifties. The fifties retained a strong sense of social stability and the moral legitimacy of our traditional institutions. After all, the United States had led the Allies to victory in World War II, which was a triumph of good over evil. As a result of the war, many became educated through the GI Bill and economic prosperity was on the upswing everywhere in America.

The sixties, on the other hand, became America's decade of cultural revolution.[6] Historian Sydney Ahlstram described the '60s as "a decisive turning point in American history." Columnist George Will called 1968 "perhaps the worst year in American

---
6 Os Guiness, *The American Hour,* New York: The Free Press, 1993, 91.

history" and the sixties "the most dangerous decade in America's life as a nation." David Potter described the sixties as

> One of the severest cases of social estrangement that any society ever experienced ... perhaps the most aggressive rejection of dominant values that any society has ever permitted without seriously attempting to curb the attack and without really defending the values under assault.[7]

Robert Nisbet relates the pervasiveness and ubiquity of the '60s for American society:

> I think it would be difficult to find a single decade in the history of Western civilization when so much barbarism—so much calculated onslaught against culture and convention in any form and so much sheer degradation of culture and the individual—passed into print, into music, into art and onto the American stage as the decade of the nineteen sixties.

Civil rights and the Vietnam War were lightening rods of change. Both led to a greater skepticism of traditional institutions and their authority. Institutions of our society were no longer seen as good, instead they became known as "the system" or

---

7 David Potter, *History and American Society*, New York: Oxford University Press, 1973, 387-88.

The Ensuing Chaos

"the man." Traditional ideas of morality, civic behavior, religion, and authority were all under attack. Technology, especially television, enabled everyone to see what was happening each day on the evening news. Unlike revolutions of the past, however, this was not a movement of the oppressed.

The civil rights struggle was for blacks to share in the prosperity of white America by having equal opportunity and respect. The sexual revolution of the sixties was a manifesto for a new morality. The Vietnam War brought about protest from young people who saw no sense in a conflict George F. Kennan described as "the most disastrous of all American undertakings over the 200 hundred years of its history."[8] All of these revolts teamed together to create a crisis of cultural authority that extends to this very day. Institutions were not under siege for being merely outdated but for being irrelevant to a new way of living. As Guiness puts it:

> the counterculture revolt was of the unoppressed, a response not to constraint but openness. It was a rich kid's radicalism.[9]

---

8 Guiness, *The American Hour*, 100.
9 Ibid, 99. Guiness does assert a positive role of the '60s revolution in that "it protested effectively against mindless materialism, hypocritical moralism and intellectual equivocation,"[97]

45 Years into the Wilderness

This was not a political revolution changing the way of governance, but a social revolution in which there would be a radical departure and discontinuity from moral, religious, and social ideals in America.

Part of the loss of cultural authority, as it has expanded, can be laid at the feet of the institutions themselves. While the Civil Rights Act of 1964 was a corrective to ensure equity, since that time the executive branch through its unelected bureaucracy, has enacted program after program that has changed equity to preference. The Civil Rights Movement's success emboldened public interest groups to push for liberation from all perceived repressive classes and categories. Creating "minority" status for blacks, women, and now homosexuals has done nothing but increase hostility and place the government in an untenable position of compromise. Privileged status by fiat trumps merit. The state has lost the virtue of being impartial and thus the moral authority to make impartiality the law for all.[10]

The violence of the 1960s at colleges and at the 1968 Democratic National Convention in Chicago were effective tools of influence against government and universities. To this day, authority has been on

---

10 Jacques Barzan, *From Dawn to Decadence*, (New York, New York: Harper Collins, 200), 764.

The Ensuing Chaos

the defensive, always concerned about the populism of the masses. Now, in the twenty-first century, many of those on the outside in the sixties are now on the inside of the institutions. As students, they wanted to get rid of Western Civics, as administrators they now have. All of this began in the Seismic Sixties, which began the changes we see today. Changes that were, in the view of Guiness, "potentially as significant as any in nearly four hundred years." [11]

The first full decade to follow the graduation of the class of '65 introduced the world to OPEC, a force still to be reckoned with today. Everyone also learned of a building in Washington, DC, the Watergate, which became the by-word for a scandal that directed a further blow to the institution of government. There also emerged a new category of political belief—neo-conservative. These were in the words of the movement's godfather Irving Kristol, "liberals mugged by reality."[12] A renewed interest in religion also emerged as many "hippies" of the six-

---

11 Guiness, *The American Hour*, 101.
12 Ibid., 110. Neo-conservatives were much in the forefront of the Presidency of the 43rd President, Geo. W. Bush, reputed to be the architects of the strategy of democratization of the Middle East and especially for the conflicts in Afghanistan and Iraq to further that ideal.

ties became part of the seventies "Jesus Movement." Jimmy Carter, as President, identified himself as a "born again Christian" and 1976 was christened the "Year of the Evangelical" by *Newsweek* magazine.

But the revitalization of institutions was not a byproduct of all this. Religion began, or continued, its descent into private expression and individualism. Although Richard Nixon had resigned in shame, his chastening did not lead to reinvigoration of government. The aforementioned Jimmy Carter won the presidency from Gerald Ford in 1976, but his ineptitude in handling the economy and the first real Iranian hostage crisis made him a one-term president.[13] The "me-ism" that helped fuel the turbulence of the sixties was beginning to take a new turn. The prosperity that permitted the baby boomers to be rebels against "the system" was about to take center stage again through economic conservatism.

The twentieth anniversary of the graduation of the class of '65 was in the middle of what Os Guiness calls the "Empty Eighties." Under Ronald Reagan there were seemingly "happy days again." The

---

13 Ford had stepped up to the presidency after Nixon resigned, but his pardon of Nixon played no small part in the lack of confidence the voters showed at the polls.

The Ensuing Chaos

inflation that had been the scourge of the Carter administration lessened. Under Reagan's leadership, Communism fell as a political/economic system symbolized by the Berlin Wall that was dismantled in 1989. Employment was up but so was the national debt. Prosperity was at an all time high, but as many argued, at the expense of the future generations. Even amidst all the economic highs, however, there was no return to traditional morality, religion, and authority. The crisis of authority could not be solved economically.

In many ways, the economic revolution of the eighties was built on the cultural revolution of the sixties. The sixties redefined our social beliefs and the eighties our economic beliefs. Lee Atwater, one time chairman of the Republican Party, said the eighties were about acquiring wealth, power, and prestige."[14] A change as great as the revolution of the 1960s occurred. There was a combining or melding of the "right" to do my own thing and the social and economic life of the individual. Anything goes, whether behaviorally or financially, as long as it is based on an individual exercising his "rights." This increasingly became the public philosophy of all

---

14 Guiness, *The American Hour*, 126.

45 Years into the Wilderness

folks, whether called conservatives or liberals. It was also the tapping of the gusher of "rights" that flows forth today.

As the 1990s dawned, a cultural fault line was appearing, partly brought on by the presidency of Bill Clinton. He and his conduct seemed to breathe new life into the idea of returning to the Golden Fifties. As the first sixties generation president, and having "not inhaled" when he smoked marijuana, he reintroduced America to the idea of differing values for differing folks. The sixties rent the moral fabric, the seventies enshrined the me and the eighties made our end health, wealth, and pleasure. It appeared that in Clinton the country was confronted with the results. Some liked it and others did not. The cultural divide became established.

On one side was the liberal/secular type... embodied in Bill Clinton. They represent the restructured, transformed America that rid itself of the old, useless structures allowing us to be all the better and freer. On the other side were the conservative/religious (or those at least not hostile to religion) embodied in Rush Limbaugh. They wanted to reject the disjunction of the sixties and return to the earlier traditional social values and structures because America today is poorer and weaker for throwing off its traditional values. It was People for the American Way versus Focus on the Family, ACLU versus ACLJ, gay marriage versus traditional marriage, and Blue State versus Red State America. This culture war was and is, in many ways, the delayed reaction to the revolution of the 1960s.

The coming of the new millennium was shadowed by fears that our technology could not cope with a year not starting with the number one. The year 2000 came with fanfare but without catastrophe and all eyes turned to the Presidential election. George W. Bush, a Texas governor, defeated the incumbent Vice-President Al Gore with fewer popular votes, but with an Electoral College majority. Gore sued and the case was decided by the U.S. Supreme Court in Bush's favor. This did nothing to dampen the culture wars because Bush was a cultural conservative, Gore a cultural progressive. The acrimony over the election lost its fervor on September 11, 2001 when, with the crash of airliners, America was attacked by a new kind of enemy.

The attacks on the United States on what would forever be called 9-11 became an event burned into consciousnesses like Pearl Harbor and the assassination of President Kennedy. No one will ever forget where they were when they received the news.

45 Years into the Wilderness

Although the aggressors represented not a nation, but an idea, the War on Terror soon became battles fought by U.S. soldiers on foreign soils. Homeland Security became the largest federal bureaucracy and "security" was elevated over personal rights.

Bush became a wartime President and the war in Iraq became a political issue similar to Vietnam. Protests of a sort not seen since the 1960s erupted. Even when the United States, unlike in Vietnam, finally took control of the situation in Iraq, the involvement in the war became an issue in the 2008 Presidential elections, fueled in large part by protesters who were the "60s people" and their heirs. LBJ quit, Bush did not, but the protesters would elect someone they believed would get the United States out of Iraq.

Then came the second cataclysm of the first decade of the new millennium...the financial meltdown of 2008–2009. Called by some the Second Great Depression, it was an unprecedented loss of confidence in a financial system that had multifaceted causes and lead to trillions of dollars of lost wealth for individuals and corporations. As I write this page, it is still uncertain how long it will take to recover from the economic shockwaves. What is now known is that the federal government has become involved as never before in banks, insurance companies, and auto companies and has the greatest federal debt in history through bailing out companies and through spending to try and put folks back to work.

Together with the war issue, this economic dive lead to the election of the first African American president, Barack Obama. Just forty-four years after the Civil Rights Act, America had a black president. It is an amazing story, and one the country can be proud of. Just look back at Chapter One and what was happening in the south as the class of '65 was set to begin their senior year. What is more significant in the long run may be Mr. Obama's agenda of "change," much of which hearkens back to the '60s and the Great Society. Capitalism is in disrepute; socialism or social justice through redistribution has new life. There is nothing new under the sun, only old ideas happening to new people. The 1960s, it seems, never go away or out of vogue in the consciousness of progressive America and Americans.

Historian Paul Johnson summarizes how the 1960s legacy has haunted us to the present day:

> Viet Nam and its bitter sequel, the Great Society and its collapse, that Imperial Presidency and its demolition: these constituted in combination, a

suicide attempt of the West. They were powerful factors in ending the great post-war economic expansion and returning international society to the fear and disarray of the 1930s. Equally important, they undermined the capacity of American leadership to respond to the new instability.[15]

Reagan cured some of the problems in the eighties, but the American leadership necessary to respond to instability based on moral, social, and religious certainty is still lacking. As has been seen in the last few presidential elections, the struggle over Supreme Court nominees, judicial and legislative maneuvers over homosexual "rights," and the culture of death issues of abortion, stem cell research, and mercy killing, there is no consensus of social virtue any longer. The economic crisis and the continued problem of "securing the United States" in an increasingly unbalanced and radical world gravitate the country's leaders away from any attempt to achieve a social consensus. The majority desire economic freedom and safety. That is where leadership is demanded, not on social, ethical, and moral issues.

---

15 Paul Johnson, *Modern Times*, (New York, New York: Harper Perennial, 1992), 658.

The Ensuing Chaos

The old ways are gone thanks to the forty-five years since the 1960s. Trust in institutions and standards have been replaced by trust in self. The chaos begun in the 1960s has brought us to where we are today. We are still haunted by the '60s and the class of '65 is in the middle of it all. America is a land of fractured institutions, families, and virtues. Everything has seemingly changed. How did this all happen? Why did chaos follow the graduation of the class of '65? Can we connect the dots?

Why the Chaos? Connecting the Dots

It is easy to chronicle what happened since the class of '65 walked away from commencement as newly minted high school grads, but why did it happen? How did it come to be that all of what eighteen-year-olds knew as cultural rights and wrongs melted into oblivion? It seems safe to say that the lack of cultural authority today stems from the radical individualism birthed in the 1960s. Like any movements, however, it did not just happen. Movements begin with a concept that comes to fruition in action. As a preacher once said: "Adultery does not just happen, it comes from an idea or desire hatched on the inside." So it is with cultural change, it is not autonomous…it has a genesis in an idea.

During the senior year of the class of '65, the *Courier-Express* reported some of the obvious changes. The Civil Rights movement and the Vietnam War were subjects brought to the attention of everyone, including those in DuBois, but there were deeper currents running through the culture. Multiple revolutionary movements were afoot. They were enunciated as one in the famous term "counterculture." This phenomenon was an "effort to discover new types of community, new family patterns, new kinds of sexual mores, new kinds of livelihood, new aesthetic forms, new personal identities on the far side of power politics, the bourgeois home and the Protestant work ethic."[16]

According to historian Gertrude Himmelfarb, the revolutionary movements led to an overall cultural revolution that embodied many aspects. Included in this revolution was:

> a racial revolution (inspired by the civil rights movement); a sexual revolution (abetted by the birth control pill and feminism); a technological revolution (of which television was a notable by-product); a demographic revolution (producing a generation of baby-boomers and a powerful peer culture); a political revolution (precipitated

---

[16] The idea of the "counterculture" was introduced by Theodore Roszak in an article in the March 25, 1968, issue of *The Nation* entitled "Youth and the Great Refusal."

Why the Chaos? Connecting the Dots

by the Viet Nam War); an economic revolution (ushered in by the Great Society and the expansion of the welfare state); and what might be called a psychological revolution (the "culture of narcissism," as Christopher Lasch dubbed it).[17]

The result was a change in culture fed from multiple sources that led to rejection of all the authorities, institutions, behaviors, and understandings that were once accepted. While the class of '65 may not have understood or appreciated what was happening, they were breathing the rarified air of the overall revolution.

Awareness of these revolutions came in drips and drabs. When I was a student at Penn State, the college football team was on its ascendancy in national recognition under their new coach, Joe Paterno. Mega-concerts at Rec Hall were part of the celebration of victories. The Supremes, Temptations, and Four Tops entertained thousands of fans through 1967. In 1968, a change occurred. The fall concert headliner was Big Brother and the Holding Company with their lead singer Janis Joplin. From Motown, a music of choice from my high school days, to hard rock in twelve months! To quote Stephen Stills, then

---

17 Gertrude Himmelfarb, *One Nation, Two Cultures*. New York: Vintage Books, 2001, 17.

45 Years into the Wilderness

of Buffalo Springfield: "There's something happening here." Shortly thereafter, a war protest magazine, *The Garfield Thomas Water Tunnel*, named after the Naval Ordinance Laboratory on campus, appeared with a cover photo of a naked John Lennon and Yoko Ono. Even a kid from DuBois could not miss that the culture he lived in was changing.

While I was at law school in Pittsburgh the antiwar movement moved from images of Chicago and Kent State. Law students, the very fodder for keeping the system of "the man" going, were joining in the rebellion. Colleges all over Pittsburgh were closing for a protest rally downtown. My classmate, the late Jack Knight, and I rode his motorcycle down to the protest and marveled at how these college students, young people like the two of us, could bring the colleges in the city and the city itself to a halt. I certainly did not grasp the enormity of the revolutions Himmelfarb catalogued thirty years after the fact, but it was then I came to realize that change had come and was continuing to come to my accustomed way of life.

A loosening of moral restraints and discipline also occurred in the lives of Americans. This aided an increasing self-indulgence and hedonistic behavior that led to enslavement to passions and/or

Why the Chaos? Connecting the Dots

substances, not to freedom. The so-called liberation of the '60s revolution also led to the dissolution or abandonment of virtues that had heretofore bound folks together in a coherent, stable manner. Whether or not the revolutionaries intended it, the "new order" of things was no order at all. It led to chaotic social behavior. As Himmelfarb points out, it is no coincidence "that the rapid acceleration of crime, out of wedlock births and welfare dependency started at just the time the counterculture got underway." [18]

In the 1990s, looking back at what happened, Daniel Patrick Moynihan described the social situation that ensued from the counterculture revolution that began in the '60s as "defining deviancy down." Syndicated columnist Charles Krauthammer, coined a correlative term "defining deviancy up," for when behavior once believed to be deviant was accepted as normal.[19] This is seen in the twenty-first century where sexual promiscuity and preference is seen as an individual right and choice that is protected by

---

18 Ibid., 18.
19 For a full treatment of these two concepts see Daniel Patrick Moynihan, "Defining Deviancy Down,," *American Scholar*, Winter 1993, 17–30 and Charles Krauthammer, "Defining Deviancy Up,," *New Republic*, November 22, 1993, 20–25.

the state. The sexual component of the cultural revolution has led to abortion on demand as the right of a woman protected by the state (*Roe v. Wade*) and homosexual activity that likewise is the right of consenting adults (*Lawrence v. Texas*).

When the class of '65 was growing up, such "rights" were unheard of. In fact, the institutions and authorities of that time prohibited abortion and homosexuality. The cultural revolution has turned the situation upside down. Sexual activities seen as wrongs or perversions are not seen as such any longer. Authority is now used to enforce what was formerly prohibited. The old sexual mores defined within the traditional family have been overturned. No longer is conduct fostered or deterred by the traditional family. In Rozsak's formula, a new concept of family, community, and sexual mores has been established by the counterculture.

This change is seen in all the other parts of the revolution. The racial revolution extended beyond equality to preference. Being black translated into "preference" in admission to the academy and "set asides" for labor and management positions in the workplace without concern for merit or performance. This has created a social circumstance in which successful blacks are often viewed as products

Why the Chaos? Connecting the Dots

of a system rather than individuals who have proved their mettle through achievement. In its most malignant form, the black preference has manifested itself in a call for "reparations" to current blacks for the slavery of their ancestors. This was a reflection of the idea of the correctness of diversity. No longer would America be the melting pot for that was really invidious discrimination against all ethnic minorities. With authority and institution no longer important, or characterized as control by the political elite, what became paramount were the individual and his or her individual identity. So, whites should pay blacks for the sins of other whites against blacks in the past. This became more important in the new ethic than homogeneity and assimilation into one nation.

Technology had just begun its dominance in the '60s. Himmelfarb is correct to point to television as a corrosive force in the counterculture revolution. Neil Postman has chronicled how television changed people from readers and thinkers to entertained and manipulated responders to images and sound bites that shape our "feelings" about all things.[20]

---

[20] Neil Postman, *Amusing Ourselves to Death*, his book on television turning viewers into non-critical thinkers. See also, *Technopoly*, Postman's withering

45 Years into the Wilderness

It is no mistake to call it the "boob tube" for it turns the viewer into a thoughtless boob. The avalanche had just begun. Copy machines, facsimile machines, personal computers, microwaves, portable phones, digital libraries and music, the Internet, iPods... technology marches on, all for the purpose of making the transmission of information and our lives in general easier. All these advances made it seem like a better world and masked the loss of shared virtues that once provided stability to our communities and relationships. Technology abetted "doing your own thing" and made that appear as the only virtue.

The sheer number of baby boomers dictated much of what has happened. Their numbers made the counterculture the majority movement. The institutions and authorities were helpless against the relentless press of the new ethic by the young Turks who came to dominate the culture. Aided by the "Greatest Generation" wanting their children to have more than they do without having to sacrifice to do so, the baby boomers threw their efforts into changing the very ethos that made their anti-establishment positions possible. Never-ending

---

critique of technology in general and its negative consequences for us all despite its prompters touting technology as all good or at worse, neutral.

Why the Chaos? Connecting the Dots

technological advances made it seem like no big deal to discard the "old ways." The new way became the narcissistic way of self-gratification enabled and fueled by our gadgets.

The political facet of the revolution was aimed at changing the authoritarian structures and institutions that lead to war and conflict. The "Military and Industrial Complex" as well as business in general was to be rejected. The new way was the inclusion of all minorities into prominence...racial, ethnic, gender, and sexual. As a result of Watergate, the inclusion was supplemented by exclusion. The political elites, represented by Nixon and his henchmen, were those who must be neutralized in politics. Thus was born a new populism, one powered and motivated by the counterculture and all of its anti-authoritarian individualism. This placed political muscle behind the idea of social, ethnic, and sexual diversity.

The economics of the countercultural revolution lead to more government. It is true as Himmelfarb notes that the Great Society was the cornerstone of the cultural revolution. The government was going to put an end to economic disadvantage just as the Civil Rights movement had ended racial inequality. This was the working out of what became the liberal politics based on diversity, the changing of authority, and the new cultural ethic needed to replace the personal ethic. Liberal politics were a moral effort in the public square to bring about social and racial justice. This did not include the personal morality and virtues of the past. The old ways of family and business were rooted in bigotry and intolerance and so must be rejected.

So, a George Wallace, who argued that the radicalism of the revolutionaries of the 1960s was out of touch with the values and concerns of ordinary folk, was dismissed as a bigot playing on racial fears. Here we see how the various impulses of the revolution worked together. The economics of the advantaged (business and capitalism) had to be reversed. The majority of poor folk were black and that was because the economy of the past was discriminatory. It required a massive program by a government that now understood that the diversity of the individual must be maintained. Any argument to the contrary was based in the racial bigotry of the old ways and must therefore be disregarded. The proper role of the institution was to make everyone equal on all bases for that was the only way to insure social justice. The pre-revolution ways of politics, recognition of individuals, and economics were immoral and must be ignored and jettisoned.

Why the Chaos? Connecting the Dots

All of this emphasis on the individual and personal autonomy could only lead to the "culture of narcissism" described by Lasch.[21] The 1960s escape from authoritarian social structures gave rise to individual "liberal values" that transcended common virtue rooted in community, family, and institution. The revolutionaries focused on the individual because of the corruption and bigotry of traditional community, family, and institution. This countercultural revolution razed the past and erected a present built on the narrow foundation of the individual. It was a new and unprecedented way of trying to establish a society. When all the dots are connected, it reveals each of us as individuals, standing alone.

The countercultural warriors wanted significance without duties, liberation but not purpose, freedom to do and be as they like without limitation of any kind on the individual. How could there be a consensus built on individuality? How could there be meaningful community? These folks adopted a stance that prized individuals as members of ethnic, racial, gender, or sexual groups. Any consensus based on institution or community was considered

---

21 Christopher Lasch, *The Culture of Narcissism: American Life in an Age of Diminishing Expectations*. New York: W.W. Norton, 1979.

unnecessary. You had your own personally chosen identifiable group of individuals. Politics was only valid to level the playing field among individuals in their non-institutional groups so that socially and economically they could all be equal. This individuality threw the former institutional and traditional consensus and stability into chaos.

Thus shaped, this radical individualism was based on ethnicity and gender as well as personal morality individually created and adopted. The class of '65, like all who followed, descended into this void of individuals plus nothing. Behaviors unknown to their forbears…abortion, multiple marriages, open homosexuality, addictions of all manner…were practiced and accepted. Moral boundaries provided no precedent; all were left to do what was right and proper in their own eyes. The influence of what used to be retreated in the face of individual want and desire. "I," "me," and "my" trumped all other modes of reference and identity. Pursuit of personal happiness and self-actualization to the exclusion of anything else became a way of life. This '60s view of the individual and his authority over all things left us all vulnerable to the corrosiveness of massive movements beyond any individual's control.

We Are All Modern People

The slightly built Frenchman careened through the door of the car breathlessly. The tall handsome Italian Ambrose was preparing a tray of tea and cakes served on silver and porcelain as only The Orient Express did. "Ambrose," gasped the Frenchman, "Do you know who is in my car?" Not waiting for a reply, he announced proudly, "Rene Descartes." Not turning from his work the Italian dismissively replied, "So." Exasperated, the younger man spat forth, "RENE DESCARTES!" and after a pause, "the great French mathematician and philosopher." And, again before waiting on a reply, the excited Frenchman said, "What shall I do?" As he turned to exit the car with his tray, the tall man said coolly, "How about your job. See what he would like to be served, Pierre." Pierre acting like that was an idea he had not considered, smiled to himself and returned the way he came in to the preparation car. He nervously approached Monsieur Descartes in the club car down the aisle from behind him. He moved by and turned smartly, facing the French genius. Descartes looked up at *the fellow countryman from behind a book. Pierre quickly asked, "May I bring you some tea and cakes, compliments of The Orient Express?" Without any emotion Rene Descartes replied, "I think not" and immediately disappeared!*

This little piece of fiction is not at all funny if you are not familiar with Descartes' famous phrase *cogito, ergo sum,* "I think therefore I am." Descartes was by all accounts a Christian, but his famous phrase began the promotion of faith in reason. Man had always used reason, but here there is an attempt to place all knowledge in the realm of ideas that are abstract and assumed to be true. Faith in this type of reason is rationalism. Rationalism says that analytical reasoning is the sole avenue to truth.[22] Descartes paved the way for modernism born of the Enlightenment.

The idea of reason drove the Enlightenment as no other idea did. In France, the essence of the Enlightenment—literally, its *raison d'être*—was reason. "Reason to the *philosophe*," the *Encyclopedie* declared "is what Grace is to the Christian."[23] Modernism came out of the Enlightenment working its way through the fields of human endeavor like art,

---

22 *From Dawn to Decadence*, 200-202.
23 Gertrude Himmelfarb. *The Roads to Modernity*. New York: Knopf, 2004, 18–19.

architecture, literature, and philosophy. A common phrase to announce modernity was: "God is dead and man has come of age." Modernists rejected the supernatural but retained the idea that truth, justice, beauty, and other ideals could be formulated but only through humanist ideas derived by reason, science and technology. This entailed a break with what was heretofore known and embraced. It followed that whatever was old "is obsolete, wrong, dull or all three."[24]

Permanent freedom from the past and all authority, including God, was at the center of the Enlightenment Project. The enlightened modern man was skeptical, rebellious, and responsible for what he believed because he was an independent and intellectually competent individual. Meaning and morality were firmly in the hands of man. Reason replaced revelation and men were the shapers of reality. Modernism, at its core, is an attitude of great self-confidence. Man by his reason can be and accomplish all things.

David Hume agreed that belief in miracles was irrational, but he was no friend of science either. Hume claimed the mind learns everything from

---

24 *From Dawn to Decadence*, 714.

45 Years into the Wilderness

experience and our cause and effect view of things is not really a system that can be called science. Immanuel Kant tried to rescue science from Hume and in so doing created a category of things we can know and one of things we cannot know. Science was in the former as truths that could be known in space and time. On the other hand, religion was in the category that could not be known. Kant did assume the existence of God, however, for meaning in life. Nevertheless, these men were firmly in the modernist camp notwithstanding questions about science by Hume and Kant smuggling God in the back door.

This was not only an academic enterprise. In the 1960s we all became modern people.[25] How did that happen? Two words come to mind…progress and technology. Our world in modernism was defined by progress and technology. They were the concepts of truth we could rely upon. When the baby boomers came into the world, there was no doubt about the fact that their lives would be better than their forbears, the Greatest Generation. That was a given.

---

25 I am indebted to David Wells, former Professor at Gordon-Conwell Theological Seminary and Professor Eric Miller, Professor of History at Geneva College for helping to shape my thinking on how we all became moderns.

We Are All Modern People

There was no end to the progress in sight, and that progress was fueled by technological advancement.

Technology gave us the opportunity to disregard the old ways because it was helping us to overcome space, time and nature. In the United States, capitalism was the perfect economic system because of its innovations for profit and ability to mass produce goods that lead to a better life for all. Affluence and comfort became the pursuit of the modern life. It was a materialistic, self-focused way of living. Newer, faster, more efficient, bigger, better, just plain more became the passwords of production based technology. Progress was the end without regard to the results or consequences. Whatever the juggernaut of technological progress produced, it had to be good for us.

Modern man became consumer man. Technology was constantly creating demand for the "latest thing," the "newer and better widget." Advertising converted wants into needs. We see the outworking of that today where two-thirds of our economy is based on consumer spending. This consumption mentality began in the '60s. I can remember seeing the Rose Bowl Parade on the first color television in my neighborhood on New Year's Day 1963. It was not very long until everyone had a color TV. Why?

45 Years into the Wilderness

Because you had to have one, and now, most households have more than one. But shouldn't you have a bigger set, a flat-screen set, or one that is high-definition? That is the way the production-oriented capitalistic system driven by technology works. A product is introduced, demand is created, and the product is constantly refashioned to be "better" and "essential."

Everyone became a modernist through consumerism. We bought into the idea that life consists in what we have. Modern advertising abandoned the former goal of merely calling attention to a product and promoting its advantages. Now, in the words of Lasch, advertising was itself a manufacturer:

> Advertising serves not so much to advertise products as to promote consumption as a new way of life. It educates the masses into unappeasable appetite not only for goods but for new experiences and personal fulfillment. It upholds consumption as the answer to age-old discontents of loneliness, sickness, wariness, lack of sexual satisfaction.[26]

Everywhere modern man turns, he faces encouragement to consume and participate in the latest

---

26 Lasch, *The Culture of Narcissism*, 72.

technological advancement. Our life became "stuff," stuff we had and stuff we wanted. There became no higher purpose in life than consumption and we sought personal fulfillment and completeness by purchasing the latest offerings of Wal-Mart, Macy's, L.L.Bean, or Lord & Taylor.

Pursuit of ease, comfort, and pleasure became the essence of our existence and were accomplished by consuming and accumulating. We were "progressing" through our lifestyle, which was a perfect answer to the rejection of the traditions and virtues of the past. It was the hedonistic grasping of the new and shiny; our participation in the truth of progress and technology. This is how the everyday man became a modern man. We no longer needed to be discerning people seeking wisdom of a higher calling or purpose. We were looking for personal happiness and entertainment through "stuff." This was the new order that emerged after throwing off the old order.

So, as the class of '65 came into the world man was the authority and his reason was all that was needed to explain the world. The wisdom and tradition of the past were rejected as pre-modern ideas to be liberated by the new maturity of modern man. An unwavering faith in science, technology, and

45 Years into the Wilderness

progress promised to always make life better. The members of the class of '65 were breathing deeply the air of modernism, whether they knew it or not. There was nothing that we could not accomplish. After all, we were conquering space and all sorts of diseases, providing more goods and prosperity than ever before, and working on a unified theory of physics. We soon would be able to explain everything and do anything. Modernism fed the ego of the radical individual and created what turned out to be unreasonable expectations.

Two world wars and a depression had shown cracks in the modern framework, but the view persisted that man would conquer all through technological advancements and lead a life of unchecked happiness. The limitless horizon for accomplishment through science and technology, and success defined by wealth and all of its trappings, was embraced as the new gospel by the class of '65. The chaos that followed 1965 did not only cause great social upheaval, but the modernism into which man had firmly planted himself also came under attack

Let Me Introduce You to Postmodernism, the New Us

Modernism sowed the seeds of its own destruction. The Enlightenment project could not deliver what it promised. Never-ending progress has not panned out. The greatness of the human has crashed upon the rocky shoals of reality. Man cannot work his way out of misery, trials, and tribulation by using all that progress and technology can produce to consume. Reason alone cannot deal with the categories and realities of evil and sin. A culture built on consumption is shallow and vulgar, producing few people of character with commitment to anything outside themselves. Such a culture did not provide a foundation upon which to build an objective world view. In the words of Philip Reif, it was a culture built on "the superiority of all that money can buy, technology can make, and science can conceive."[27] Modernism was collapsing.

It is extremely difficult to determine the beginning and end of ages/periods of human history. Historians and sociologists commonly use benchmarks from the French Revolution (1789) to the fall of the Berlin Wall (1989) to mark the inception and end of modernism. Whatever the case, it is clear that during the last twenty years the Enlightenment project has ended. Postmodernism has replaced modernism. Is it a new impulse or is it just the "logical" (such a word may be a no-no) working out of failed modernism? Whatever its genesis, it has some obvious components.

All of history has been a struggle between truth claims. While modernism retained a concept of truth, postmodernism believes truth is created not found. It is a construct of the powerful and conquerors against the weak and oppressed. Truth, therefore, is relative to where you live and who is in charge. There is no one truth but many truths. As a result there is no overarching story that tells the truth. Those were just tales of control. Little individual stories are all that is left so we have your truth

---

[27] Philip Reif

and my truth. Further emphasis falls on the individual. Whatever makes him or her "feel good" or "happy" is what counts. This relates to our individual story, so we must make it good. Therapy, adjustment to what makes us feel good, is the key to individual well-being, and that is the only kind. There can be no authority except me, so all authority outside of self dies. With me as the authority, morality and ethics are self-defined so there are no boundaries for behavior. Any kind of shared vision is lost.

Modernism was a way of understanding the totality of the world in which we live. Man would figure it out with the aid of his reason through scientific truth. Postmodernism says using the reason of man to understand the world is over reaching. Views of "your" world are possible, but not more than that. All is privatized. There is merit in the attack on Enlightenment thinking as a sterile, unbiased, or neutral way to reach certainty. The postmodernist argues that all of life cannot be reduced to some kind of "one fits all" reality. No universal truth, no definition of right or wrong, no boundaries or rules are applicable across the board of human existence. Such an exercise is the arrogance of modernism. The self was untethered from the past in modernism, permitting autonomous man equipped with reason, to establish truth empirically. Now, in postmodernism, man is freed from objective reason allowing truth and morality to be determined on a personal and subjective basis.[28]

The postmodern has rethought the nature of rationality and how it works. This produces, in the phrase of John Franke, a "chastened rationality." This "chastened rationality" dispenses with the idea of an objective vantage point for viewing the world. We are all situated individuals who bring not objectivity but subjectivity to how we see things. This new rationality also dispenses with "meta-narratives" to explain life. Instead, "local" stories explain each person's view of the world. The all encompassing explanations, scientific or metaphysical, that at one time shaped modern society are no longer credible to the postmodern. All ideas of reality are local to a situated individual and there is no rationally driven,

---

[28] It is sometimes asserted that for postmodernists there is no truth or morality. That is not the case. All postmodern people are interested in truth and morality from their own perspective. They only insist there is no truth or morality of a universal nature. This, of course, begs the question: Is that not a universal statement? And, if so, is it true?

Let Me Introduce You to Postmodernism

overarching story that ties them together or subsumes them.[29]

It is easy to see how this postmodernist world view exacerbated the revolutionary trends of the 1960s. While individualism slipping from the authority of institutions was the hallmark of the '60s, there were still some overarching claims to the good, the true, and the beautiful. Now, however, that is all passé. It is individualism turned to radical individualism. It is anti-authoritarianism turned to anarchy. We have individualism on steroids! There are no shared stories, ideals, virtues, or community values...it is my truth, my way, my meaning, my business, and no one can tell me how or what to do.

Meaning and purpose come only from one's pursuit of significance and/or power in a world devoid of standards of morality outside your own. You define everything. This has become the legal and political definition of freedom in the United States according to the U.S. Supreme Court:

> These matters, involving the most intimate and personal choices a person may make in a lifetime, choices central to personal dignity and

---

[29] For an "enlightening" discussion on postmodernism see *Christianity and the Postmodern Turn*, Myron B. Penner, editor. Grand Rapids, MI: Brazos Press, 2005.

autonomy, are central to the liberty protected by the Fourteenth Amendment. *At the heart of liberty is the right to define one's own concept of existence, of meaning, of the universe and of the mystery of human life. (Planned Parenthood of Southeastern Pennsylvania v. Casey,* 505 US 833 (1992), emphasis added)

Few of us sit down and consider how this modernism morphed into postmodernism impacts us on a daily basis. Yet, what it has produced in conjunction with the rejection of the traditions and institutions of the past that permitted the flowering of radical individualism, has had a profound effect. It has produced what I will call "the new society" in which we all now live.

The New Society

It would be preposterous to doubt that we now live in a society entirely different than that in which the class of 1965 was raised. Let us look together at what the radical individualism spawned by the "revolution" of the sixties, aided by modernism, exacerbated by postmodernism, and fueled by unchecked technological progress and consumerism hath wrought as to our society.

Self has replaced human nature. This is certainly not surprising. The surprising part is that self in this new society is not seen as new or a problem. As philosopher Alasdair MacIntyre points out, "the individual" is not a natural type of human being. The individual self is a construct of modernity. We cannot escape the human condition. The self is no substitute for human nature regardless of how hard we try to make it so.

It is understandable why modern man wants to escape human nature and create the self. It permits one to believe he is free of all those constraints human nature brings—tradition, authority, religion, meaning, and nature itself. All those influences on a human being by virtue of "being" are rejected or bypassed by the self. The self reduces all the constraints on human nature to empty concepts that are only given meaning by the self. For instance, if the self wants to be "religious," he embraces religion in a manner he desires it to be for him. No religious institutions or traditions are binding on him. The only religion that has meaning to him is that to which he consents or constructs. That is the autonomy of the self.

Western society has always had a version of the self. In fact, Christianity, which provided the moral and ethical grist for Western culture, has a high view of self. That is because all selves are created in the image of God. That is the real basis of "self worth" in the West. Furthermore, to buttress the importance of human nature, God became a man in Christianity. Thus, every human being must always be treated with respect commiserate with their dignity as a human person.

The difference between the modern self and the classical Christian self is that the latter is not autonomous and a self-creator. Every human person is created for a purpose; he/she does not create their own purpose. The constructed self is individualistic;

The New Society

human nature is universal. Thus, the self had to be created to escape the universality and tradition of the human being. This self responds to the religious impulse of human nature with self created spirituality. The religion of modern man is personal spirituality. He creates what he believes and decides how to practice his belief.

The ascendancy of the self can be seen today in the lack of "virtues" as opposed to only "values." Virtue implies a universal cultural good that is passed on through tradition.[30] A virtue, such as thrift, also has a corrclative, such as waste that is not a virtue. There is an affirmation of a good and a denial of what is not good. In the Middle Ages, seven virtues paralleled the seven deadly sins.

Values, on the other hand, represent an individual placing worth on an item. Originally, a commercial term, it has now become the currency of the modern self. Wells points out that the term "value" is of recent vintage with no such entry found in

---

[30] Theologian David Wells defines virtue as "moral norms that are enduringly right for all people, in all places in all times." *The Courage to be Protestant*. Grand Rapids, MI: Eerdmanns, 2008, 143. As the discussion on modernism and postmodernism reveals, such universal virtue is no longer accepted.

45 Years into the Wilderness

the *Oxford English Dictionary* of 1928.[31] What each "values" is good simply because he values it. This has the benefit of denying nothing. What you value as good may not be what I value as good. That is the beauty of self-created value over universal virtue—it's all good!

Unlike virtue, value has no overarching application. A self chooses what he deems good just as he chooses ice cream flavors. This is an ideal way to avoid tradition. Not that "traditional family values" are not good. It is just that some "value alternative family values" are just as good as those of the past. What used to be virtues are now replaced with constructed values that meet the requirement, desire, or convenience of the self. The sovereign self is in control of all aspects of life and how it is to be lived without the inconvenience of any authority, structure, belief, or practice of the past that may be contrary to what the self values.

The self has special significance in the United States. The revolutionary sixties helped lead the populace into preoccupation with self. Lasch observes:

After the political turmoil of the sixties, Americans have retreated to purely personal

---

31 *The Courage to be Protestant*, supra, 146.

preoccupations...what matters is psychic self-improvement; getting in touch with their feelings; eating health foods; taking lessons in ballet or belly-dancing; immersing themselves into the wisdom of the East; jogging; learning how to "relate;" overcoming the "fear of pleasure."[32]

It is also the perfect vehicle for the democratic ideal of the "pursuit of happiness." Rieff predicted this in the sixties. There would be no authority except the self and personal freedom would be the basis of happiness. How can the self be happy unless the self is in charge of his happiness? It is the political right of the self to pursue his happiness.

Where is the happiness, one may ask? We live in a neurotic time in which more people are on antidepressants than at any time in history. The self is a neurotic self. The self is empty; self surfeited on its own desires. I love banana cream pie but if that were all I ate, I would be reduced to a toothless diabetic with no strength to do anything but gorge myself with pie. The self pursuing its own happiness is just as destructive as my pie eating. There is no higher good to which to aspire; no standards to which to adhere; no purpose to life outside my own

---

32 Lasch, *The Culture of Narcissism*, 4.

selfish desires. Not only is this destructive to the self, it is destructive to society because there is nothing beyond self.

This brings us to the second feature of the new society. *Community has disappeared.* The class of '65 grew up in a defined community. Different associations existed within the overall community, but there was an understanding of being a part of a greater whole. Today's dislocation is a function of the self-enclosed, subjective self. The very character of the modern self requires refusal of all involvements with substance or meaning outside self. Community associations such as churches, social clubs, and nonprofit charitable organizations decline in membership because they are not conducive to self-expression.

Associations in a community become merely a resource to be exploited by individuals. Can a community association lead to recognition or self-fulfillment? If so, it may be worth our effort. Society is reduced to a quid pro quo, a place of contractual relationship where each self benefits one another in interaction. The institutions of society are reduced to a collection of various selves in relation to one another. They are no longer desirable for purposes that do not result in self-recognition.

The New Society

Sacrifice and service for others has disappeared. Disasters still bring out selflessness in individuals, but daily living is almost devoid of doing for others unless it has self-referential benefits. Men and women are not encouraged to subordinate their needs and wants to the needs of others. We are not disposed to give ourselves to a cause or way of life outside our own "felt needs." As Lasch put it in 1979:

> "Love" as self-sacrifice or self-abasement, "meaning" as submission to a higher loyalty—these sublimations strike the therapeutic sensibility as intolerably oppressive, offensive to common sense and injurious to personal health and well being.[33]

Being driven by personal well-being in all we do eviscerates community.

Deterioration of community can also be traced to losing "place" to "space" through technology. In the Aristotelian sense, place is a concrete, particular, related to definite points of reference idea. Most of the class of '65 lived a good part of their pre-graduation lives in DuBois or the surrounding area. It was our place. We lived in neighborhoods where we knew our neighbors. Families worshipped together,

---

33 Lasch, supra, 13.

played together, and shared one another's joys and sorrows. We lived in homes—not always owned—with our families and a working parent[s]. It was not perfect; some really struggled, but it was the place we lived together.

Today, in the new society, the emphasis is on space, not place. Technology has shrunk the world. Now we are really citizens of the world not our community. We are interconnected like never before. Is it true, however, that a man can be a citizen of the world? Can you literally call earth your home? That is a fiction. We, as finite human beings, must live in a specific place at a specific time. We cannot just take up space. Space has no identity. It is an interchangeable concept without human meaning. It is amorphous, perfect for molding it into what the self wants, detachment from responsibility to all others but self. To be a citizen of the world makes everyone, but actually no one, your neighbor. Such an arrangement is self-deception that only results in separation and loneliness.

The idea of space over place has all kinds of consequences. We all witnessed one of them during the recent financial crisis. Home used to be a place, a place to live as a family. Home ownership, however, became something other than having a place for raising a family. Homes became nothing more than an investment. People used their homes as banks. Houses were purchased as an exploitable resource, not as places to live as a family. Technology and innovation made possible the bundling of pieces of mortgages and using them for investments to be securitized and sold worldwide. When the "housing bubble" burst, these investments went bust, too. The concept of home was made into an economic term without a concrete, definite point of reference. Thousands, if not millions, of these "homes" were abandoned and became worthless investments. No community can be made out of placeless investment homes only used as cash cows to further our personal consumption goals.

Loss of community also resulted in a rise in the power of the state. While this may seem an odd connection with the sovereign self, it does make sense. The state has fostered modern individualism. It has come between individuals and traditional authorities associated with community: church, family, associations, local authorities. Through the power of taxation, the state has created programs and institutions that cannot be matched by community-based institutions. The treasure chest of the state from taxation is far larger than the community purse of resources. The local communities of today have far greater financial dependence on the state and federal government than the mayor and city council of DuBois could have imagined in 1965.

The state has also become the champion of individuals against community-based institutions that suppressed their individualistic desires. What were once practices and lifestyles long frowned upon are now behaviors justified and enforced by the state. The largesse of the state has been used to aid individuals who, in theory, could not aid themselves. In very little of life does the state not have a say in how life is to be lived. With financial, judicial, and police power, the state has unfettered the individual self from all restraints to freedom. The state has enshrined the individual above all but itself. The state has created and permitted rights for the individual making itself the sustainer and guarantor of those rights.

The state has helped create a new society, a society of an indiscriminate mass of individuals. This concept of the centralized state is antithetical to community. Such a society is not a community of individual members each using their talents and efforts with a commitment to work for the betterment of the community. It is the role of the state

The New Society

to make things work. This new society is not a community at all. It is a collection of equally endowed individuals mediated by the state, the only institution that can do so. Democracy today is my right or preference to do what I want and it is through the power of the state that is accomplished. Individuals are encouraged to believe that the only important social grouping to which they belong is the state.

We are brought to the third principle of the new society. *Choice is the new right.*

Choice is the new god. Isn't life about choices? We choose our President, our deodorant, our spouse, our lifestyle, and our values. This idea of choice in all things includes moral decisions. Choice makes no distinctions and is all about immediacy and pragmatism. It is the verb that most accurately describes the self unconcerned with community and encouraged by the state.

Living as individuals of our own creation, unbound by any historical reference point, unencumbered by anything we do not "choose," results in choice being the ultimate human good. How could it not be? Choice has no bounds. Man is not precluded by any authoritative antecedents or principles, for there are no such things. Any want or desire of the individual is capable of being translated into a

45 Years into the Wilderness

"personal right" to be pursued. In addition, an individual has the state to abet the "pursuit of happiness."

In his book, *When Choice Becomes God*, F. LaGard Smith sets forth how personal choice becomes the creed of the new society:

> Having no grand vision about what life is all about, we are reduced to making ad hoc decisions based on opinion polls, media propaganda or unabashed self interest.[34]

Choice is about the exercise of the radical individualism that permeates the new society of self without community. Where there are no community virtues, restraints, or boundaries; where there is an unfettered right to create our own rights that are unchecked by societal norms, then, "anything goes."

Nothing is more representative of personal choice than abortion. In fact abortion proponents have for years adopted the label pro-choice, which certainly sounds better than pro-abortion. The gist of the position is that it is the mother's right alone to choose whether to have an abortion. Aided by the U.S. Supreme Court, abortion has been the centerpiece of the choice agenda. The exercise of advocacy through the judicial system is a hallmark of

---
34 F. LaGard Smith, *When Choice Becomes God*. Eugene, OR: Harvest House, 1990,35

The New Society

the individualism of the age and how it interfaces with personal choice. A choice that is not universally embraced or is frowned upon cannot be established through the legislative process. It has therefore fallen to the federal courts, who have been more than willing to make an unpopular choice into an individual right.

In *Roe v. Wade,* the U.S. Supreme Court determined in 1973 that a woman's fundamental right to an abortion is inherent in the Constitutional "right to privacy." As the whole world knows, the word "privacy" is not in the U.S. Constitution. It is a construct of the U.S. Supreme Court. In *Planned Parenthood v. Casey*, the court revisited *Roe* nineteen years later. It reaffirmed the "privacy right" to an abortion as a fundamental right, but readjusted how to review abortion cases. Instead of the trimester tests of *Roe*, the court adopted the "undue burden" test. Government action to restrict abortion is an "undue burden" if it purposes or effectively places a substantial obstacle in the woman's path to an abortion. Inhibiting a person's choice in the new society is not permitted.

Jeffrey Hart, professor emeritus of English at Dartmouth, sets forth an argument for the new society squarely sitting on the unfettered rights of individuals:

45 Years into the Wilderness

> Roe relocated decision-making about abortion from state governments to the individual woman and was thus a libertarian, not liberal ruling. Planned Parenthood v. Casey supported Roe, but gave it social dimension, making the woman's choice a derivative of the woman's revolution. This has been the result of many accumulating social facts, and its results already have been largely assimilated. Roe reflected, and reflects, a relentlessly changing social actuality.[35]

Note that Dr. Hart believes that the individual, personal choice for a woman to have an abortion is a social fact that has been assimilated into our culture. We are a pro-choice people as a result of social progress. It is a part of the new society.

This is indicative of the social change that was brought about by the cultural revolution of the 1960s less than thirty years after the class of '65 graduated. If Hart is correct, what was once a crime, or at least considered a sin, is now an accepted cultural fact. For the class of '65 an out-of-wedlock pregnancy brought public and private shame. To eliminate the baby would only compound the shame into a heinous act. It would be compounding the sin.

---

35 *WSJ Opinion Journal*. December 27, 2005 (www.opinonjournal.com)

The New Society

A young girl "in trouble" always had the baby. It may have been put up for adoption, but the baby would not have been aborted. I can unequivocally say that I never heard of an out-of-wedlock teenage abortion until I was well into adulthood. The choice to abort a baby being left to the discretion of the young woman carrying the child is a sea change in the morality of the culture in which we live.

Nothing seems to stand in the way of an individual's choice. Is there any societal check on behavior in the new society? The U.S. Supreme Court has cast a dark shadow of doubt on such a proposition. The case of *Lawrence v. Texas* struck down a Texas statute criminalizing sodomy. The majority actually cited the dissent of Justice Stevens in *Bowers v. Hardwick*, the Georgia case upholding a similar statute just seventeen years prior. In overruling *Bowers,* Justice Kennedy, writing for the 5-4 majority, states:

> The fact that the governing majority in a State has traditionally viewed a particular practice as immoral is not a sufficient reason for upholding a law prohibiting the practice.[36]

---

[36] For a more complete discussion of the impact of *Lawrence* and how, in the view of Justice Scalia, it could be the death knell of all legislation based on community standards of morality, see William C.

45 Years into the Wilderness

Majorities in individual states no longer have the ability to establish moral norms for their communities. It is for the U.S. Supreme Court, as arbiter of the new society, to determine what is beyond the pale, or whether there is a pale. This loss of community replaced by personal choice calls into question whether there is any common good or culture to which we all adhere.

A system of personal "goods" chosen by persons without communitarian influence leaves no public good. We are left with a collection of private goods all competing for recognition in the public square. What a crushing burden for the individual. He dictates to self what is good but without the institutions or traditions to make his private good a public good. The consequence is a dysfunctional society, one in which there are "no limits." There can never be a higher purpose; no framework for understanding an overall good...no culture.

Living for self has no regard for posterity or predecessors. We lose the sense of historical continuity. The notion of belonging to a succession of generations in a place where ideals and concepts for living were developed is disappearing. Local communities

---

Kriner (2005) "When Rights Become Wrongs," *SGM Magazine* 1:4.

The New Society

decay and local history and knowledge dies or is forgotten. Without accessing a past, what was true, good, and beautiful has no impact on the future. A crisis of authority and restraint results from not leaning on the past but only leaning on self. Thus arrives the fourth marker of the new society...*no shared culture.*

The idea of submission to a higher purpose or meaning outside self is the prime casualty of the new society. We have achieved what Reif called an anti-culture—the opposite of culture. Culture is about restraint. The new society is about liberation from all the now condemned restraints. Lasch puts it this way:

> These conventions [of Western culture], now condemned as constricting, artificial and deadening to emotional spontaneity, formerly emphasized civilized boundaries between people, set limits on the public display of feeling, promoted cosmopolitanism and civility...They shared a common fund of public signs which enable people of unequal rank to conduct a civilized conversation and to co-operate in public projects without feeling called upon to expose their innermost secrets.[37]

---
37 Lasch, 28

45 Years into the Wilderness

By establishing their own moral order and lifestyles outside of tradition, community, or institution, individuals leave no room for a shared culture. No agreement exists on the conventions and public signs that establish and maintain a culture.

A culture represents an ordering, a context in which a community lives. Constructed over time, it is an accumulation of ideals, understandings, folkways, mores, practices, rituals, and narratives. It establishes the tradition and history of the community. It represents the very concepts rejected by the autonomous self. Culture represents limitation. Where man is the measure of all things, there can be no prospect for limiting his choices. The self cannot be told what to do. No framework of understanding can form a culture when it is all about me.

The political wrangling of the Red State/Blue State types is indicative of the lack of a shared culture. There are deep chasms between what folks believe. Political conversation today lacks civility. Statesmen who hold dear to their positions yet recognize the viability of their opponent's position and seek a political compromise are in short supply. What exists is a cram down/demonizing way of establishing public policy and law.

The New Society

    We have the political power of the imperial self. When in control, look not to the good of the country…there really is not any. Look to pursue what you "value" as good. A politics that is based on every man being entitled to what he thinks is good, is reduced to sheer power and expediency. What other outcome can result from a system with no shared public good. Here is a reason why it is extremely dangerous to identify with no community except the state.

    The late Sam Francis held to the idea that right thinking about the state and culture requires decentralization, privatization, and localization. Just the opposite seems to be occurring. The federal government is becoming bigger and taking on more of what the private sector used to do. The state seems to have the same insatiable appetite for authority as the individual. Is a clash inevitable? It is at this point where the imperial self is sowing the seeds of its own destruction. For with no mediating, restraining, or ordering of individuals by a culture, the destruction of the self is assured. Unfettered, unprincipled, and unsound choices made by the sovereign self cannot continue indefinitely. Eventually a restraint will come…will it be from a once benevolent state turned despot to save the individual from himself?

45 Years into the Wilderness

Without a culture, this new society is unsustainable for another reason, what Reif calls the "therapeutic state." The United States has more psychiatrists and psychologists than any other nation in the world. That is not surprising. In a world of disconnected selves, who cares about you? If you are the creator of your own moral universe and you fail, where do you turn? If you are in charge of the way you live and you crash and burn, what community can you turn to for help?

Look around and see the hurting folks in the world. There is alienation, hostility, and indifference in a world of selves. People crumble every day in the face of adversity. When all we have to look to is ourselves, and we cannot provide the solution, we disintegrate. From our analyst, we seek mechanisms to cope, including anxiety altering drugs. When nothing changes; we just try and muddle through. Freedom to be the sovereign over your life, making your rules, acting without limitation, doing as you like, is great when the sun is shining and the band is playing. In the hurricanes of life, however, you are left in the wind and rain alone to try and survive.

Without cultural restraints and supportive communities informed by that culture, the result is what Rieff calls the "un" or "shriveled" self. That is, a society of unhappy, cutoff, neurotic, anxious people.

The New Society

Not exactly the grand and glorious outcome predicted for the autonomous self. This is the new society in which we all must live. It is populated by the imperial self, unrestrained by tradition and community, with unfettered choice to do and believe as he desires without direction from any source but self. A new society built on individual and unlimited freedom. Such a society leads to many questions. Can such an anti-culture last? From whence will order come? What can we do about any of it?

Time for Reassessment

Bewilderment...n. 1. complete confusion; perplexity. 2. a bewildering maze or tangle

This is a time of bewilderment. Nothing is like it was, and nothing is staying the same fast. The majority of those in the class of '65 were born in 1947. That was before TV, which was in the beginning black and white on small screens. It was before polio vaccine, pantyhose, wireless phones, instant coffee, and contact lenses. Hardware was found in a store and software was not even a word. Green was a color not an attitude. Spaceships were only in science fiction books. Homes had no dishwashers, clothes dryers, or air conditioners. At the office there were no conference calls, video conferencing, facsimile machines, personal computers, copy machines, or business trips to China. Ping was a noise not a golf club; all baseball was played with wooden bats; swimming was in mud ponds not concrete ones; and cars, clothes, and toys were made in the United States.

45 Years into the Wilderness

We have all made and can make lists like the one above. The purpose of such an exercise is not nostalgic recounting, but rather to realize how much has changed and is changing. What is harder to understand is how we and the world we live in have changed. There is much confusion and perplexity in the world forty-five years after the class of '65 graduated. Much of it results from a forty five year trek into a cultural and societal wilderness. What can be done about that confusion and complexity?

In preparing to write this book I asked many folks many questions. A list of some of these questions is found in Appendix A. I asked these questions because we all live busy lives. Our lives are scheduled so as to achieve maximum "productivity," whether in distraction or work, during our waking hours. Such living leaves little time for reflection about why we live the way we do. Combined with the dumbing down of discourse and learning that is apparent to even the casual observer, little thought is put into the "whys" and "wherefores" of life.

No one who answered the questions doubted that change had occurred since 1965. To a person, each recognized the complexity and confusion that marks living life today compared with just twenty years ago. Some commented that the answers they

Time for Reassessment

would have given in 1964–65 seem not to be relevant today. A lack of permanence and continuity since 1965 seems to be an accepted cause of the complexity and confusion experienced in life in the twenty-first century. As a result, many were looking for a simpler life, while recognizing the need for stability, structure, and coherence to avoid the relativism that dominates modern life.

Time marches on, for us as individuals and collectively. We are not going back to "the way it used to be." So, answers to the complexity and confusion of living life in our new society have to be an issue of the "now." Presently, we in the class of '65 and those following need to reassess "how" and "why" we are living life today. Going forward in each of our lives, an assessment of where we are and where we want to be has to be carried out to address the current complexity and confusion. What can be done to bring clarity to the confusion and simplicity to the complexity? Can there be individual peace and harmony in our lives in spite of the bewilderment of the world we live in?

A place to begin a reassessment is in examining the focus on self...nothing is more important than me, myself, and I. Philosopher R. J. Snell posits a solution to our fixation with self by reversing the idea that the world and all that is in it consists of "objects" to be used and defined by us. In a world of objects, the focus is necessarily on me and how I use the objects for my perceived good. There was a time when things were subjects, whether a sunflower, an animal, or a natural resource. These subjects had a purpose in themselves; they had a form, nature, and essence. Now these subjects are objects…objects to be used and determined worthy by another subject, man. The "choosing self," as we have seen, is a definition of modern man and he determines the use, worth, and purpose of the object. The imperial, majestic self is the new orderer of the objects because the objects no longer have form and order in and of themselves.

This subject to object progression has been a recipe for disaster and has brought about the commoditization of all things. It fits the modern and postmodern outlook chronicled above. Man no longer sees himself part of a larger order. Disengaged from his human nature as the self, and seeing the world as objects for his benefit, man has arrogated to himself the autonomy to determine the order of all things. The worth and integrity of any and all things in the world is determined by the radically autonomous agent…self. This is a self with no limitations and no standards. If this imperial self does espouse standards such as "save the world" or "feed

Time for Reassessment

the hungry" these are entirely objective. The self can send a check or support the government or a non-government agency to accomplish the goal. This avoids the messiness of dealing with subjects who may interfere with his autonomy, yet allow him to believe he is improving the lives of others.

Here is step one in addressing the confusion of the new society and reassessing our part in it. Each of us must examine how we look at the created order. Do we view it as ours to use as we see fit? Or, do we admit to limitations on our autonomous self? Do we see what is in the world as being created with subjective intrinsic worth as part of a whole where purpose comes from outside of us? This is not an argument for pantheism. We are not of equal value with a lady bug. Man is the crown jewel of creation and has been given dominion over the created order. With authority, however, comes responsibility. The authority is not to turn the created order into objects of man's desires and preferences. Man is human in nature, and part of a larger cosmic order, not the self-legislating self over and apart from that order. He is limited and ordered by something outside himself.[38]

---

[38] While this is not the place for arguing over how nature, including man, arrived in this world,

45 Years into the Wilderness

We must return to a concept of nature where man, although separate and apart from nature, treats all in this world as subjects. Only then will we begin to see limits on the autonomous self. Included in this must be the idea that subjects are worthy in themselves and are not defined by their usefulness to man in his quest for ease, comfort, and pleasure. This should also temper choice as the only ultimate good. At the very least, we will not look at what we choose to do or think based on our self. The world will have meaning again and man's role in it regulated by recognized order and limitation. Something more is involved here than just satisfying the desires of the self. Man is again engaged with the world, a world with meaning outside of consumption and self-satisfaction.

The autonomous self also objectifies other human beings because they are a threat to a selfish existence. With the tempering of choice as god,

---

nevertheless, this is an Achilles heel of any sort of naturalistic or materialistic view without order. One adopting a non creation position must necessarily expect tooth and claw, survival of the fittest and exploitation of the strong over the weak in their random, accidental nature for that is reality from a cold, impersonal set of forces without meaning or order.

Time for Reassessment

there is also hope for community and culture. This is the second step in reassessing how we want to live in the new society. When purpose is not found in self, there is no longer a need for competition among sovereign selves. Instead, opportunity develops for a sense of community in which individuals come to see the need for limitations and standards. It offers an alternative to the pursuit of self-interest and self-fulfillment, what Wendell Berry calls the individual life that "implies no standard of behavior or responsibility."

Community requires a commitment to ones other than self in service and sacrifice. It means coming to an common understanding about the place where you live, the virtues that you share, the symbols that represent who you are in cooperation, the beliefs that underpin how you live and the meaning of it all. It takes priority over the imperial self seeking meaningless diversion or entertainment as an expression of freedom. Community offers an active suppression of self in favor of membership with its spirit of selflessness, sense of belonging, and satisfaction of cooperation.

Substituting self-gratification with communitarian impulses also re-establishes the worth and significance of others. Treating others as meaningful subjects may even result in an appreciation for community life. Berry defines this as when neighborly love, marital fidelity, local loyalty, the integrity and continuity of family life, respect for the old, and instruction of the young are valued. Not many would say the foregoing list represents ideals and behaviors not in themselves good. These community virtues have, however, been neglected or lost as a function of the rejection of the history and tradition that spawned them. These ideals are clearly not compatible with the solitary aims of the self-serving individual.

Transitioning from self fulfillment to community fulfillment will not be easy. For it requires a willingness to join in with the sorrow and joy of a community—as specific people in a specific place—in particularity of their needs, failures, and triumphs. Such a world no longer revolves around selfish desires. It means living out the traditions, rites, and customs of the people closest to you with tears and laughter. The self becomes part of a human endeavor where no individual creates his own experiences but rather shares life with others. The individual is enriched because his universe is no longer defined by his personal reach. This is an authentic, meaningful life not a delimited life of separation and loneliness.

Time for Reassessment

To achieve community goals over and against individual desire takes an act of the will whereby the importance of place, tradition, and history are elevated above self importance. Pursuing community involves the bigger goal of living in a shared culture. That is, the continuity and harmony of living from one generation to the next. The community transmits the folkways, mores, beliefs, ideals, institutions, traditions, and higher purpose that represent a culture. Through community, that culture is shared. Human beings, understanding their common humanity, and no longer seeking self-centered purposes, can and will learn to place themselves under a culture that limits individual behavior. Just as the autonomous self did not arise overnight, this process too will take time.

Moving toward a renewed appreciation of the individual as a human being and part of something greater than oneself permits a reassessment of what it means to live a flourishing life. This is step three in examining where we are and how we live. The society where the sovereign self exercises his freedom without restraint defines human flourishing as an "experience" of personal satisfaction. It must be so. For to the self, experience is everything. It was not always so.

45 Years into the Wilderness

We have addressed modernism and postmodernism. In pre-modern time, man understood God as the only source of good things. Only God could make a man good and happy. Life was centered on God and not on circumstantial experience. With the eighteenth century and the onslaught of modernism, it was determined that human flourishing was a project, not from above, but from below. No longer did we need to acknowledge something outside ourselves in order to understand human flourishing.

Even the new modern project of human flourishing was still tied to others. Even if we need no longer love God (whatever it may be), we still loved our neighbors. There was a connection of community…human flourishing was tied to one another and was not a solo flight. As we moved from modernism to postmodernism, however, the universality, the togetherness of human flourishing, was lost. It was becoming a solitary act capable in aloneness. As discussed at length above, others were only good or useful in so far as how they served our personal happiness.

The cultural move to the autonomous self fit hand in glove with the concept of human flourishing based on experiential satisfaction. In the *ancien régime*, it was love of God and neighbor. In modern

Time for Reassessment

times it was the universal love of man. And in postmodern times, it is the personal experience of happiness; self-love alone. Today, the desire to be happy remains, but love is gone…love of God and fellow man. There is only me. R. R. Reno calls this the "Empire of Desire." It is the selfishness of desire in the age of autonomy.

We have witnessed a total avoidance of fitting oneself into any larger reality for the sake of human flourishing. Human flourishing, however, cannot solely be about self if there is to be community and culture. It is time we once again examine the meaning of life. What is life all about? Is personal happiness the only result that counts in living life? Is life without love for anything outside self, life outside community with no requirements of service and sacrifice, and living without being bound to the traditions and standards of a culture, all there is? Until we realize that we are slaves to selfish autonomy without community or culture, we cannot come to an alternative view of human flourishing allowing us to fit in to a larger reality. We are left with the Empire of Desire with self-serving choice as its only virtue.

The fourth part of reassessment we all must make is questioning the importance of consumption as the primary expression of living today. "We are what we consume" has become the mark of modern and postmodern man. As noted above, the commodities available for consumption are endless. The nationalization and internationalization of economies has only increased the choices, and has resulted in the further weakening of our localities. Individual workers and families are no longer important to the economy except as consumers. Economic decisions are increasingly centralized, leading local communities to decay and become unimportant to the wellbeing of community members. Local folks become dependent on international corporations and state and federal bureaucrats for their economic wellbeing. This affects everything in the community.

Education is no longer a local matter. Sure, there are school boards but they operate under state and federal mandates. The purpose of education is no longer based on cultural inheritance or succession. It is to prepare young ones for new and better jobs. Invariably, those jobs are not found in the local community. Children are educated to leave home, and they do. Education is now for "success," as in personal success, wherever it takes you. After all, you are the focus of education, not how you fit into a grander scale for the benefit of a community or culture.

Time for Reassessment

The casualty of economic centralization is the local community, its continuity, history, integrity, memory, and culture. Community is disposable and changeable without any permanence or commitment. The only thing that is important is the economic system determined from afar. When the class of '65 graduated, DuBois was a place where you could purchase what you needed from local merchants. There were men and women's clothing stores, grocery stores, drug stores with soda fountains, hardware stores, furniture stores, jewelry stores, and local banks all owned or controlled by residents of the community. Now there is Walmart and malls with businesses paying minimum wage and taking the earnings out of the community.

Prosperity and privacy are other recent phenomena of the consumer-based culture. It used to be that only kings and potentates could have private prosperity, and it was usually built on the backs of the less fortunate. Today, there is widespread prosperity through technological advance and the proliferation of goods for everyone. Not everyone is Donald Trump, but almost everyone has access to transportation, televisions or computers, and cellular phones...mobility, entertainment, and communication. Every individual can be buried under a multitude of goods and services through personal consumption. Unlike any other time in the history of man, we experience individual consumption and the unencumbered, personal enjoyment of commodities, all in the privacy of our own space and time.

This mentality of consumption permits the consumer to ignore or avoid any responsibility to a community or public life. The perception is that the original indicia of human frailty, lack of food, clothing and shelter, is not at issue any longer so each is free to consume himself to ease, comfort, and pleasure. Of course, the premise of this position is flawed. There are those in the United States without adequate food, clothing, and shelter. It is a commentary on our consumer society that folks on food stamps or government payments of some kind have iPhones and iPods. Having the latest gadgets, whether rich or poor, is how folks are socially graded. No matter your economic status, the individual self, seeking personal satisfaction through consumption, is the paradigm for twenty-first century man in the United States. Such a self is the perfect fit for the new society.

Unbridled consumption for personal satisfaction impairs our capacity for human flourishing, keeps

Time for Reassessment

us from wholly integrating into community and culture, and defines us as shallow depthless human beings. Do we individually want to live like that? As human beings, not consuming imperial selves, we can be about something more than having the latest iPhone. As a member of a community we can care about the real needs of others among whom we live life and share virtues of a common culture. All of us must reassess whether our time and treasure is only to be expended on us. None of us are going to change the national and international economic system. Yet we can be more than our material possessions. In the end, we can conclude that there is more to life than being a consumer.

What Now?

If the reassessment suggested in the prior chapter leads you to reconsider how you are living your life in this new society, there arises a new question. What now? What can one do to combat the bewilderment and confusion of the present age? How does one reconnect with our humanness in culture and community and flourish as a human being without being focused on self and stuff? It seems pretty clear that the era of the autonomous self will have an end. When and what will be the result is unknown. The relativism that is spawned by the Empire of Desire results in lack of order and coherence in the new society. Today, everything goes. No society, however, can continue to exist as a collection of individuals without common cause or purpose.

We will never be pre-modern people again, but we can reach for a concept that integrates an appreciation of the created order with a concept of human flourishing built on something other than personal happiness. It will not be easy, but it can be done… one person at a time. It begins with understanding that human flourishing is not dependent on economic success. Life is not measured by a continual movement upward in material worth or status. The entertainer, professional athlete, and Wall Street banker do not represent the epitome of human flourishing. While that may be the spirit of the age in which we live, no one need buy into that idea on an individual basis.

Human flourishing can be on a farm in Nebraska or in Calcutta tending those dying and discarded on the streets. A life of service, sacrifice, and hard work can be a rewarding life. We cannot be carried on the tide of progress by technology into believing that gaining ease, comfort, and pleasure through consumption is the only pursuit compatible with human flourishing. Great reward may be found in living, working, and loving local, simple lives without capitulating to the world around us.

Next, we need to recapture the idea of being part of a greater whole. We are not islands of personal desire. We must again learn to love in community; be part of something greater than we can ever be on our own. This can be a powerful antidote to the new society around us. Meaningful life can result from "little platoons" in the words of Edmund Burke. Communities formed not to benefit us, but to benefit others, be they churches, social clubs, associations, or neighborhood groups. Doing for others has the exhilarating tendency to shift focus from the self to our common bond as human beings. A common purpose permits the pursuit of a common good and goals that are far more rewarding than selfish ambitions. Pursuing community life allows for a sharing of sorrow and happiness not possible in the pursuit of a solitary life. Lived in community, life is robust and fulfilling, a contrast to the insular and petty self-centered life.

By belonging and submitting to community, we come to understand that as a part of something greater than the self, there are also restraints and standards to which we are bound that are not self-created. There are ideals, standards, rites, mores, folkways and morals that are normative for communities. When we belong, we confess our willingness to be placed under an authority that is for the good of the community. The autonomous self becomes the responsible self.

Finally, we can no longer consume ourselves into happiness and out of responsibility. Must we become monks or ascetics? No, but we are to be prudent and responsible in the use of our resources. We must reject the idea the "we are what we consume." When we overcome our self-seeking and come to appreciate that flourishing as a human being is not limited to accumulation of material wealth, power, or prestige, we move away from a superficial expression of life through consumption. Resources can then be used not for selfish satisfaction of personal desires, but rather to assist and aid others in your community and culture, especially the least of these. This results in a deep and communal life of engagement with the world around you instead of a shallow and isolated life of distraction from all but self.

The way we live can no longer be unexamined. Failing to do so allows one to be carried along in life by the tide of confusion and complexity spawned by our new society. There must be a reassessment of what is occurring in the society in which we live. That analysis must also examine and help us to understand our relationship to this world in which we live. Are we individuals seeking the best for us in all matters; defining our own reality and basis for living without limitation? Or, are we part of a greater whole with a contribution to make for the good of all, limited by something outside ourselves? We can escape from the bewilderment and confusion of the new society, but to do so we must seek stability, order, structure, and coherence for our lives and the lives of our loved ones.

This book began by trying to explain the complex set of circumstances that set in motion the new society we have today. It is not a stretch to say the 1960s represented a cultural revolution with the rejection of all that was the conventional wisdom of the time. The thesis of this work is that what began by overthrowing the old ways led to the new society of the autonomous self unfettered in any way from pursuing his/her personal desires and establishing his/her own reality. The result was the establishment of a wilderness of personal desire; the wilderness in which we find ourselves. This chapter calls for another revolt against the wisdom of the age, a countercultural movement that rejects the conventions and ideals of the new society. It is time for the new radicals to rise up and bring about a new revolution, one person, family, and community at a time. It is time to leave the wilderness.

Epilogue

As a Christian, I would be unfaithful to my calling and my Lord not to insert what I believe is the only real solution to the new society. That is the embracing of the Gospel of the Lord Jesus Christ. I understand this is not a popular solution for "problems" in our new society. In a sense, that is a justified position. The Gospel is not for solving problems or making bad folks good. It is not a solution to the ills of the world, save for one: The most dire one…sin. Sin does cause the problems of the world, makes people bad and separates us from a holy God. The Gospel…or more correctly Jesus Christ…is the answer to sin.

The conventional wisdom of today with regard to Christianity is that it is one of many ways to God. Religious pluralism is the norm. The radical individualism referred to in this book abets this. The relativism of modern man encourages belief that all religions are the same. What works for you may not work for me, so belief is relative to each person.

45 Years into the Wilderness

Religion is just another commodity to be consumed based on personal choice.

This is not intended to be a theological treatise on the exclusivity of Christianity among religions of the world. It is simply to say Jesus Christ is uniquely the way to overcome the difficulties created by the new society. The reason is quite simple. For the Christian, Jesus is the authority. Self-centeredness is no longer a problem. The life led is no longer self-centered but Christ centered. Community is no longer a problem. The Christian belongs to the church which is a community with standards, prescriptions, requirements, and duties that are not fashioned by any of us. They are Biblically based. One of those responsibilities is the obligation to be a good citizen (render unto Caesar); love your neighbors as yourself; and even love your enemies. Not much room for self-focus there.

Nor is there a problem with consumption. Christians are to be generous folks, giving to the church and their fellow man. There is no hoarding or over consumption permitted; the Christian is to be a cheerful giver and care is to be given to the "least of these." Christians are to be rule keepers. Not only are there the Ten Commandments, but also the teachings of Jesus and the keeping of His

Epilogue

commandments. Christians are to be those who are known by their love of one another.

Now, I am aware that readers will say: "I don't see these things in folks calling themselves Christians." I agree, but the poor examples you see do not make the message poor. It was G. K. Chesterton who said: "The Christian ideal has not been tried and found wanting, it has been found difficult and left untried." In the prior discussion of human flourishing, there was reference to the *ancien régime* when men were guided by the love of and for God. That is Biblical and it cannot be overthrown by any modernistic or postmodern emphasis on science and man. God is part of human flourishing and as God has been marginalized in nations and cultures, societies have become less humane. This is so in Marxist régimes and in the consumption oriented capitalism practiced on a global scale. Something else has been substituted for God and His righteousness.

This applies equally to "religious" folks of any stripe. This is demonstrated in what is called the parable of the Pharisee and Publican found in Luke 18: 9-14. There Jesus admonished his disciples that it wasn't the pious religious guy who trusted in himself for righteousness who was righteous. No, it was the tax collector who cried out for mercy as a sinner.

45 Years into the Wilderness

The regular guy, not the "religious" one, was the one right with God. It was a pretty clear message. You can only be right with God when you abandon the idea that you place yourself in God's favor by who you are or what you do.

When I was a young lawyer, everyone wanted me to join their organization… Rotary, Lions, Kiwanis, United Way, YMCA, Elks, *ad nauseam*. Why? I was a lawyer don't you know…uniquely qualified to be in their organization! Well, Christianity is the only institution where you have to be disqualified to belong. You are nothing and have nothing to present. And you can do nothing to get in. You must acknowledge your inability to belong in order to belong! Seems quite strange in this world that rewards personal accomplishment, but that is the way of Jesus. The guy who thought he was in and ok was not; the guy who knew he could not qualify, did. How? By acknowledging his inability to belong and asking for the mercy of God to make him able to belong.

In this book I have tried to speak to the need to acknowledge that we are human beings who best flourish as such in community with standards and common beliefs that serve as cohesion among us. This is what Christianity represents in this world. Also, I have tried to point out that the sovereign

Epilogue

self-animated pursuit of self interest has made choice god and consumerism religion. In Biblical parlance this is idolatry. It is the creation of a false god to take the place of the one true God. It is a pretty stark comparison: submitting to the standards and ideals of the church community of God or striking out on your own to establish how you will live based on your own desires.

The problem we confront is that dire one of sin. Even if we want to change from the imperial, self-seeking life because we see the foolishness of it, we cannot. Like the poor tax collector, we must acknowledge who we are and pray for mercy. That's where we all find ourselves...self justified or God justified. Jesus pronounced a harsh sentence for the self justified. Jesus told his disciples such an approach does not work. Why would we think it did today?

Not much Christianity is seen today because of the failure of so-called Christians to live out their faith in Christ in obedience and sacrifice. Jesus reduced all of obedience to two commandments about love (Matt 24:37-41). One, love the Lord your God with all your heart, soul, strength, and mind. In other words, love God more than your stuff, your position, your power, your family, yourself. Second, love your neighbor as yourself. In Jesus' world, there is no room for the self-centered life. For Jesus, if you love Him you keep (obey) His commandments. The proof of being a Christ follower is not what you say but what you do…not profession but obedience.

Sacrifice is also prominent in the teaching of Jesus. He pointed to the widow's mite as being greater than all other gifts placed in the treasury by the rich (Luke 21:1-4). How can that be? Because it was out of want not surplus like everyone else. She was sacrificing and was evidencing her love for God. He told the parable of the Samaritan (Luke 10:29-37) who helped and paid for the recovery of a waylaid Jew when others, of his own people and seemingly more pious, did not. This Samaritan, whom we call good, did all this for a stranger when he did not have to. Jesus uses him as a commendable example. Why? The Samaritan loved his neighbor. Sacrifice of time and treasure for others, strangers or not, is expected of Christians.

The chilling teaching about sacrifice is in Jesus' separating the sheep (heaven bound) and the goats (hell bound) at the time of His judgment (Matt 25: 31-46). Those who feed the hungry, gave drink to the thirsty, took in the stranger, clothed the naked, and visited the prisoner were rewarded for they were really doing it for Jesus. There were no earthly

Epilogue

rewards or accolades; no one knew what was being done. It was a display of loving God and neighbor at the same time in assisting "the least of these." Those who refused to assist the "least of these" showed their disdain for God and their neighbors. Their failure to obey and sacrifice indicated that they were not His sheep but goats to be condemned.

You see, true Christianity is the antithesis of the world…it is countercultural. It is more radical than the radical individualism of the new society because it is so out of sync with accepted behavior today. True Christianity is focused on the love of God and neighbor, not self. My late mother used to identify the Christian life as JOY…Jesus, others, you…in that inviolable order. Christianity is the perfect belief to lead the counter revolution against the new society.

In the new society, we see no obedience or sacrifice. The self-centered person only answers to his own desires. These folks view sacrifice as having a 36" rather than 54" plasma TV. Obedience is absent for there is no authority outside self. Sacrifice is absent because satisfying self is the goal of life. On the other hand, obedience and sacrifice are to be the marks and goals of Christian living in this world. This is what separates, or should separate, Christians from all the rest. It is how Jesus separates His sheep from the goats. When professing Christians begin living as they ought, what a different world there will be. For non-Christians, look not to what goes on in this world for expressions of Christianity. Look to what Jesus said and then look for individuals and churches living in obedience and sacrifice to and for Him.

True Christianity is difficult to practice in this world, but it is not wanting. Following the way of Jesus results in a life of obedience and sacrifice, as well as a love of God and neighbor. That is a good result for the follower and his neighbors. Just think if it caught on, wouldn't that lead to a better and different world? It would provide a remedy for the bewilderment and confusion of life lived today in the new society. There would be authority, community, shared ideals and standards, service and sacrifice for others, and an overthrow of the self as the focus of all that is done. That would truly be a revolution.

This Jesus Revolution is greater than any other revolution in history, including the cultural revolution of the sixties, in its scope, depth, and results. It is a revolution that is out to topple all human wisdom…pre-modern, modern, or postmodern. It is a transcultural revolution; it applies to folks whatever their circumstance, situation, location, or condition.

Epilogue

It works from the inside out, changing the hearts and minds of individuals. It is not a revolution to return us to the "good old days" of the class of '65. Rather, it is a revolution that gives new life, new standards, and new purpose pointing forward to eternity in the Celestial City of God. How does this occur? It occurs one person at a time who repents and believes.

Appendix A

Questions Asked

What were the defining influences in your life before and after high school?

What were the defining experiences of your life before and after high school?

How have your views changed on these questions since high school?
    Where did you come from?
    What is your authority?
    What is the purpose for your life?
    What becomes of you when life ends?

What is most important to you in living your life?

    How have your beliefs about the purpose of your life changed since graduation from high school?

45 Years into the Wilderness

What do you see as the major changes in our culture (the shared mores, morals, ideals, standards and beliefs...the way we live) since your high school graduation?

In what ways have you changed as a person since high school graduation?

Anyone reading this book who desires to answer any or all of these questions may do so by e-mailing krinerlawoffice@ verizon.net.

Appendix B

Interview with Zach Siggins and Erik Stidsen

My grandson, J. Zachary Siggins, and one of his best friends, C. Erik Stidsen, were seniors at State College (Pennsylvania) High School during the 2009–10 school year. Their senior year marked exactly forty-five years since I was a senior. This interview was conducted in July of 2009, and in it we obtain a glimpse of experience in high school as well as the future expectations of two middle-class young men at the close of the first decade of the twenty-first century in the United States.

Q: *What are you looking forward to in your last year of high school?*
ZS: Home football games.
ES: I would honestly say coming closer to knowing what I want to be when I grow up.

Q: *What is your best experience in high school?*
ZS: Taking AP history in eleventh grade.
ES: Playing high school ice hockey.

45 Years into the Wilderness

Q: *What was your worst experience in high school?*
ZS: Precalculus…would I get a good grade while not trying that hard?
ES: I didn't have an experience I would call bad.

Q: *What was your most valuable learning experience in high school?*
ZS: Staying after AP history class and talking with my teacher.
ES: My personal finance class because my teacher talked to us like we were adults.

Q: *If you could change anything about high school, what would it be?*
ZS: I agree with Erik's answer…
ES: I like school and would not change a thing.

Q: *How has high school, in your opinion, prepared you for real life?*
ZS: Our teachers do less hand holding than before in school. You have to work and you choose how you want to do. The teachers don't call your parents.
ES: The teachers let you do things on your own.

Q: *What concerns you most about what happens after this year?*

Appendix B

ZS: I am concerned about being prepared for college-level classes and professors.
ES: Getting into a good college, allowing me to have the most successful life I could have.

Q: *Have you ever considered not going to college?*
ZS: No, but I have considered taking a year off to have a worthwhile experience before going to college.
ES: Never.

Q: *Have you ever considered military duty?*
ZS: Yes, I have considered it, but I do not think I am brave and selfless enough to serve my country in the military.
ES: Not really.

Q: *What if you received a college education and did not obtain a good job?*
ZS: I try to be optimistic and have faith in my ability to get a good job.
ES: I would try and get a part-time job I liked.

Q: *Do you expect to do better financially than your parents?*
ZS: No.
ES: No.

45 Years into the Wilderness

Q: *Is that a good or bad thing?*
ZS: Every generation should be able to build on what they already have.
ES: Bad.

Q: *Guys of your generation have more stuff than any generation before you. Is that good or bad?*
ZS: We need technology to survive.
ES: I think we are too reliant on technology.

Q: *Has technology increased the stress in your life?*
ZS: No.
ES: No.

Q: *Do you intend to marry and raise a family?*
ZS: Yes.
ES: Yes.

Bibliography

Books

Barzan, Jacques. *From Dawn to Decadence* New York: Harper Collins, 2000.

Black, Jeremy. *Altered States: America Since the Sixties* London: Contemporary Worlds, 2006.

Guiness, Os. *The American Hour* New York: The Free Press, 1993.

Himmelfarb, Gertrude. *One Nation, Two Cultures* New York: Vintage Books, 2001.

———. *The Roads to Modernity* New York: Knopf, 2001.

Jenkins, Phillip. *Decade of Nightmares*: *The End of the Sixties and the Making of Eighties in America.* New York: Oxford University Press, 2006.

Johnson, Paul. *Modern Times* New York: Harper Perennial, 1992.

Lasch, Christopher. *The Culture of Narcissism: American Life in an Age of Diminishing Expectations.* New York: WW Norton & Co., 1979.

Levy, Peter. *America in the Sixties: Left, Right and Center.* Westport, CT: Greenwood Publishing, 1998.

Penner, Myron, ed. *Christianity and the Postmodern Turn.* Grand Rapids, MI: Brazos Press, 2005.

Potter, David. *History and American Society* New York: Oxford University Press, 1973.

Postman, Neil. *Amusing Ourselves to Death* New York: Penguin Books, 1986.

———. *Technopoly.* New York: Vintage, 1993.

Smith, F. LeGard. *When Choice Becomes God* Eugene, OR: Harvest House, 1990.

Wells, David. *The Courage to be Protestant* Grand Rapids, MI: Eerdmanns, 2008.

Bibliography

Periodicals

Krauthammer, Charles. 1993. *New Republic* November 22.

Kriner, William C. 2005. *SGM Magazine* Vol. I, No. 4.

Mills, C. Wright. 1960. *New Left Review* Sept-Oct.

Moynihan, Daniel Patrick 1993. *American Scholar* Winter.

Rozak, Theodore. 1968. *The Nation* March 25.

The Courier Express. Various dates between August of 1964 and June of 1965.

The New York Times. August 5, 1964.

WSJ Opinion Journal. December 27, 2005.

Reference

Dictionary of American History, 3:165.